ONE HUNDRED AND ONE HYMN STORIES

By
CARL F. PRICE

THE ABINGDON PRESS
NEW YORK   CINCINNATI

TO MISS EMILY S. PERKINS
WRITER OF CHRISTIAN HYMNS,
COMPOSER OF HYMN TUNES, AND
FOUNDER OF THE HYMN SOCIETY

031407

PREFACE

EVERY real hymn has its story, if only we could discover it. The background of the author's life, his spiritual experiences, his conflicts, his sufferings, his victories, sometimes a startling incident, sometimes a soul crisis, sometimes a season of exaltation —these things are woven into the thought and feeling of a great hymn. And perhaps, in some measure, the fact that these hymns have been wrought out of actual human experience gives to them the great power which they undoubtedly exert upon the hearts of men. Certainly, to know what conditions produced a given hymn often adds to our appreciation of its meaning and our responsiveness to its message.

Of the real origin of many of the best hymns we know little or nothing. Their story is enshrouded in mystery. Of some hymns, as the stirring missionary hymn, "Soon May the Last Glad Song Arise," hymnology has been unable to disclose even the author. "Mrs. Vokes" is the name attached to this hymn; but who knows who she was, or even what was her full name?

Of other hymns, however, much has been brought to light by patient students of hymnology. Some authors have quite fully taken us into their confidence as to the origin of their hymns, while concerning others much has been gleaned from contemporary sources.

It is the purpose of this book to present in compact form some of the most effective stories of well-loved hymns, so that without wading through voluminous works on hymnology the general reader, and especially the pastor, Sunday-school superintendent, and other leaders of worship, may have them in

5

PREFACE

easily accessible form. Some of the stories are here presented for the first time. Still more of them have been drawn from the recognized sources of English hymnology and have been retold in brief form.

The book owes its origin to a meeting in the winter of 1923 of the New York Sunday School Superintendents' Association, representing many denominations, when the use of hymn stories was discussed as a means of arousing greater interest in the message of the hymns and as an antidote to thoughtless, mechanical singing, so prevalent in Sunday schools and even in church worship. A number of superintendents testified to the great help they had found in the use of the author's previous book, *A Year of Hymn Stories,* now out of print. And an appeal was made to him to double the number of stories in that book and reissue the whole collection in convenient form. This has been done. And it is our devout hope that this primer of hymnology may help stimulate more intelligent and more worshipful use of the hymns which are such a precious heritage of the church.

CARL F. PRICE.

New York, August 29, 1923.

ONE HUNDRED AND ONE HYMN STORIES

1. My Faith Looks Up to Thee

RAY PALMER, 1808-1887

MANY of the best Christian hymns were penned by very young men. Ray Palmer, son of Judge Thomas Palmer of Rhode Island, started life as a dry-goods clerk in Boston; but after three years of preparation at Phillips Academy, Andover, he entered Yale College and graduated in 1830. He began teaching at once in New York city, and that year, though only twenty-two years of age, he wrote this hymn, which has been sung for nearly a century to the blessing of thousands of worshipers.

That year was one of deep discouragement, for it brought to him a fearful battle against illness and poverty. But his faith looked up to Christ to strengthen his "fainting heart," and while he was treading "life's dark maze," he sang:

> Bid darkness turn to day,
> Wipe sorrow's tears away,
> Nor let me ever stray
> From Thee aside.

In recounting his experiences which inspired the hymn he afterward wrote: "I gave form to what I felt by writing, with little effort, these stanzas. I recollect I wrote them with very tender emotion, and ended the last line with tears. I composed them with a deep consciousness of my own needs, without the slightest thought of writing for another eye, and least of all of writing a hymn for Christian worship."

His faith conquered, and his life was greatly blessed in wide Christian service as pastor of Congregational churches in Bath, Maine, and Albany, New York; and still later as corresponding secretary of the American Congregational Union.

7

2. Peace, Perfect Peace

BISHOP EDWARD HENRY BICKERSTETH, 1825-1906

TEN years before Doctor Bickersteth was made Bishop of Exeter he was spending the summer of 1875 at Harrogate, in a house loaned to him by the Vicar of Casterton. His son states that one August Sunday morning he heard Canon Gibbon, who was then Vicar of Harrogate, preach from the text, "Thou wilt keep him in perfect peace, whose mind is stayed on Thee." An allusion was made in the sermon to the original Hebrew words of the text which were, "Peace, peace," once repeated: the 1611 translation happily rendered these words, "Perfect peace." This fired Doctor Bickersteth's imagination and set him to thinking upon this subject.

That afternoon he called on Archdeacon Hill, of Liverpool, who was approaching death, and he found the Archdeacon troubled in mind. Eager to share his thoughts upon peace with the dying saint, and believing he could best give to him real comfort in the form of verse, he took up a sheet of paper and wrote this hymn exactly as it is used to-day, and then read it to him.

The hymn with its questions, each expressive of some one of life's difficulties, and its answers, each coupling the name of Jesus with some precious thought of comfort, has often been used in times of intense sorrow. But the Rev. S. Bickersteth, son of the author, tells us: "The most touching occasion on which, personally, I ever heard it sung was round the grave of my eldest brother, Bishop Edward Bickersteth (of South Tokyo) at Chiselden in 1897, when my father was chief mourner."

8

3. Where Cross the Crowded Ways of Life

FRANK MASON NORTH, 1850-

WHILE Professor Caleb T. Winchester, of Wesleyan University, was helping the Hymnal Commission prepare *The Methodist Hymnal* of 1905, he met Doctor North in the Methodist Book Concern building, New York city, one day in 1903 and said: "Why don't you write for us a missionary hymn? We need more hymns on that subject in our hymnal." Doctor North disclaimed any ability to write a hymn worthy of that book; but Professor Winchester, being familiar with some of his poems, insisted, and Doctor North promised to try.

Shortly before this Doctor North had preached a sermon on Matthew 22. 9, "Go ye therefore into the highways"; and being especially impressed by the rendering in the Revised Version of the words, διεξόδους τῶν ὁδῶν, "the partings of the highways," he described the appealing challenge made by the crowds of people thronging such places as Union Square and Rutgers Square in New York and similar squares in European cities where with a yearning heart he had watched the people come and go. This suggested a first line for his hymn,

> Where cross the crowded ways of life.

The picture of Christ, returning from the Mount of Transfiguration and healing a young man, inspired the lines,

> O Master from the mountain side,
> Make haste to heal these hearts of pain.

His special interest in social questions and his years (1892-1912) as secretary of the city missionary work of New York Methodism (from which he entered the foreign missionary secretaryship) find eloquent expression in this hymn, which appears in more standard hymnals than any other hymn of this century. It was first published in 1903.

4. Sweet the Moments, Rich in Blessing

WALTER SHIRLEY, 1725-1786

IN its present form this hymn was wrought out of a bitter experience in the life of Sir Walter Shirley, who was at the time Rector of Loughgrea in the County of Galway, Ireland. His brother, the Earl of Ferrars, a man of evil habits, engaged in a quarrel with one of his servants, who had long been in his employ, and in the passion of his anger he murdered the old man. He was at once imprisoned; and Shirley, though mortified by the terrible disgrace which the revolting crime had brought upon his family, journeyed to his brother's prison and remained near him during the distressing weeks that followed. The Earl was tried, convicted, and sentenced to be hanged at Tyburn. After the execution Shirley, worn out by his long vigil and humiliated in spirit, returning to his parish, finding comfort only in the cross of Jesus Christ.

Discovering an imperfect expression of his emotions at that time in a hymn, "O How Happy Are the Moments," by the Rev. James Allen, he adapted and revised the hymn so completely that it became practically a new composition, truly poetic in language and form, and tenderly eloquent of his own experience:

> Sweet the moments, rich in blessing,
>   Which before the cross I spend;
> Life and health and peace possessing
>   From the sinner's dying Friend.

Walter Shirley was a cousin of the famous Countess of Huntingdon, a devout woman who engaged in the preparation of many hymn books, in one of which this hymn first appeared.

5. Hark, the Voice of Jesus Calling

DANIEL MARCH, 1816-1909

AFTER his graduation from Yale in 1840, Daniel March studied for the ministry and in 1845 received ordination from the Presbyterian Church. Still later he entered the ministry of the Congregational Church, in which he was serving in Philadelphia at the time when this hymn was written—the only one by which he is known as a hymn-writer. He was announced to preach before the Christian Association in Philadelphia; but not long before the service he discovered that the hymn chosen to follow the sermon did not fit the sentiment of his discourse. He had selected as his text Isaiah 6. 8: "Also I heard the voice of the Lord, saying, Whom shall I send, and who will go for us? Then said I, Here am I; send me."

Full of his subject he wrote the four eight-line verses of the hymn beginning with the lines,

> Hark, the voice of Jesus crying,
> "Who will go and work to-day."

The last line re-echoes the thought in the latter part of the text:

> Who will answer, gladly saying,
> "Here am I, send me, send me."

The hymn was sung at his service from the manuscript, and formed a fitting climax to the thought of the sermon in much the same manner as George Duffield, Jr., used as a climax for a sermon his hymn, "Stand Up, Stand Up for Jesus" (*q. v.*).

The second verse seems to be modeled after a hymn, popular in that day, by Mrs. Ellen Huntington Gates, "Your Mission," which was an especial favorite of President Lincoln's, as sung during the Civil War by Philip Phillips, its first line being "If you cannot on the ocean."

6. I Love to Steal Awhile Away

PHEBE HINSDALE BROWN, 1783-1861

PHEBE HINSDALE, the daughter of the composer of the psalm-tune, "Hinsdale," was left an orphan at the age of two. A relative, keeper of the county jail, brought her up amid drudgery and cruel hardship, so that she was robbed of a happy childhood and never even learned to read until she was eighteen. During three months' school at Claverack, New York, she gave her heart to the Lord and joined the Congregational Church.

Later she married a house-painter, Timothy H. Brown, and settled in East Windsor, afterward moving to Ellington, Connecticut. Here they lived very humbly in a small, unfinished house, and with her four children to care for and a sick sister in the only room that was finished, there was no place about the house where she could be alone for devout meditation and restful quiet.

Therefore at twilight she would frequently slip away from home and walk alone along the road as far as the garden of the next house, where the fragrance of the flowers and the beauty of the sunset hour gave her opportunity for meditation and communion with God. But her neighbors wondered, and gossipers talked, and the woman who owned the garden once asked her somewhat haughtily: "Mrs. Brown, why do you come up at evening so near our house and then go back without coming in? If you want anything, why don't you come in and ask for it?"

That night, with all the children abed, save the baby in her arms, she burst into tears. Taking a pen, she wrote in verse, "An Apology for My Twilight Rambles, Addressed to a Lady," from which the verses of this hymn are taken.

7. Praise to the Holiest in the Height

JOHN HENRY NEWMAN, 1801-1890

"THE Dream of Gerontius," by Cardinal Newman, like Tennyson's "In Memoriam," Milton's
"Lycidas," and many another poem of power, was
the expression of the author's emotions and meditations upon the death of a dear friend. It pictures
the quest of the soul of a monk in his journey after
death toward Purgatory. As finally the wandering
spirit is brought into the presence of Emmanuel, a
choir of angels is represented as singing this hymn,

> Praise to the Holiest in the height,
>   And in the depths be praise,
> In all His words most wonderful,
>   Most sure in all his ways.

The author was not pleased with the poem when
completed, and threw it away, but a friend of his
rescued it, and in 1865 it was published in *The
Month,* in the issues of May and June, and met with
such immediate favor that it was included in the
author's *Verses on Various Occasions* in 1868.

Subsequently it was given a wonderful musical
setting in the oratorio, *Dream of Gerontius,* by the
distinguished English composer, Elgar.

When William Ewart Gladstone, England's
"Grand Old Man," lay dying in his home, he frequently quoted this hymn, finding in its noble sentiments a comforting solace in his last days. Canon
Scott Holland in preaching at Saint Paul's Cathedral
pictured the dying prime minister as "spending his
life in benediction to those whom he leaves behind in
this world and in thanksgiving to God, to whom he
rehearses over and over again, day after day, Newman's hymn of austere and splendid adoration,
'Praise to the Holiest in the height.'" The hymn
was sung at Gladstone's funeral.

13

8. How Are Thy Servants Blest, O Lord

JOSEPH ADDISON, 1672-1719

MANY hymns have been composed by travelers, the thought of which has been suggested by the scenes and experiences of travel. Such hymns are, "Lead, Kindly Light," "Sow in the Morn Thy Seed," and "O Little Town of Bethlehem" (*q. v.*). To this class of hymns belongs "How Are Thy Servants Blest, O Lord," written by the famous English essayist, Joseph Addison.

Lord Macaulay, in the *Edinburgh Review,* July, 1843, recounted this incident which occurred to Addison in the midst of his travels on the Continent, which extended from 1699 to 1702:

"In December, 1700, he embarked at Marseilles. As he glided along the Ligurian coast he was delighted by the sight of myrtles and olive trees which retained their verdure under the winter solstice. Soon, however, he encountered one of the black storms of the Mediterranean. The captain of the ship gave up all for lost, and confessed himself to a Capuchin who happened to be on board. The English heretic, in the meantime, fortified himself against the terrors of death with devotions of a different kind. How strong an impression this perilous voyage made on him appears from the ode, 'How Are Thy Servants Blest, O Lord!' which was long after published in The Spectator."

The influence upon English literature of this paper, The Spectator, to which Addison regularly contributed his charmingly written essays, is immeasurable. On Saturday, September 20, 1712, in No. 489 of that periodical there appeared an essay on "Greatness," which dwelt especially on the greatness of the ocean and the fondness of great painters for sea pieces, and concluded with these lines, now popularly known as "The Traveler's Hymn."

9. Depth of Mercy! Can There Be

CHARLES WESLEY, 1707-1788

"DEPTH of Mercy!" which was first published in 1740, originally contained thirteen verses, and was entitled "After a Relapse Into Sin."

Doctor Belcher, in his *Historical Notes on Hymns and Authors,* tells the story of an actress who was in a country town when she heard a group of humble people in a cottage singing this hymn. She entered and found a service in progress which she followed with the deepest emotion. After she had departed the tender words of Charles Wesley's hymn haunted her and at last she secured a copy of the hymn book. Over and over she read the words with their winsome picture of Jesus Christ, wounded for her transgressions, weeping for her waywardness, but still loving with an infinite love. And thus she was led to surrender to Him.

Her conscience troubled her about continuing her work on the stage, but the manager of the theater with plausible arguments induced her to go on with the leading part in a new play soon to be produced, and she appeared on the opening night. Her entrance on the stage was to have been accompanied by her singing of a song in the play. But the song she could not sing, for she was thinking of her recent conversion and of the hymn which had brought her to Christ. Finally, clasping her hands and with tears in her eyes, she sang to the audience:

> Depth of mercy! can there be
> Mercy still reserved for me?

10. O Little Town of Bethlehem

PHILLIPS BROOKS, 1835-1893

WHEN Phillips Brooks was rector of Holy Trinity, Philadelphia, his parishioners in August, 1865, sent him abroad for a year. His travels took him through Europe, and in December to the Holy Land. Here with reverent feet he traced the footsteps of his Lord and Master from Nazareth southward and visited the scenes of the Bible narrative.

After two weeks spent in Jerusalem, Christmas Eve found him in "the little town of Bethlehem" at the birthplace of Jesus. Of his stirring emotions on that "Holy Night" he later wrote to his Sunday school back in Philadelphia:

"I remember especially on Christmas Eve, when I was standing in the old church at Bethlehem, close to the spot where Jesus was born, when the whole church was ringing hour after hour with the splendid hymns of praise to God, how again and again it seemed as if I could hear voices that I knew well, telling each other of the 'Wonderful Night' of the Saviour's birth, as I had heard the year before; and I assure you I was glad to shut my ears for a while and listen to the more familiar strains that came wandering to me halfway round the world."

Two years after his return to America, still full of the thrilling memories of Bethlehem, Phillips Brooks wrote for his Sunday school the Christmas hymn, "O Little Town of Bethlehem," which for a long time had been singing in his soul. In this he has embodied, as in the prose descriptions of places visited in the Holy Land, the spiritual meaning of what he there saw. An Easter hymn also by Bishop Brooks, "God Hath Sent His Angels," refers to other scenes in Palestine which he visited.

11. Another Year Is Dawning:

FRANCES RIDLEY HAVERGAL, 1836-1879

MISS HAVERGAL, who wrote the famous New Year's hymn,

> Another year is dawning!
> Dear Master, let it be
> In working or in waiting
> Another year with Thee,

spent her life "in working and in waiting" for the Master. In August, 1850, before she was fourteen years old, she entered Miss Teed's school, where the influences over her were very helpful. The following year, she says, "I committed my soul to the Saviour, and earth and heaven seemed brighter from that moment." She earnestly strove to make each year after that hallowed experience

> Another year of service,
> Of witness for Thy love.

Wherever she went in her frequent travels she was constantly asking people whether or not they knew of the joys of salvation, and by thus being a witness she led hundreds of souls to the cross.

> Another year of training
> For holier work above.

Her heart was fixed upon the more glorious work, which God has prepared for us to accomplish in heaven. When, in 1878, she was taken seriously ill, and was told her life was in danger, she replied: "If I am really going, it is too good to be true!" "Splendid! To be so near the gates of heaven."

This hymn was written in 1874 and was first published as a New Year's card, later in collections of her own works, and finally in many hymn books. It has proved to be an inspiration to thousands standing at the threshold of a new year.

17

12. Just as I Am, Without One Plea

CHARLOTTE ELLIOTT, 1789-1871

MANY unsaved souls imagine it is difficult to come to Christ. And this at first was the thought of Charlotte Elliott, the author of this hymn. Shortly after she became an invalid, with a helplessness lasting fifty years, Dr. Cæsar Milan visited her father and talked with her concerning her soul's salvation. At first she rudely resented this, but afterward repented and asked him how she might find the way to Christ. He replied: "Dear Charlotte, cut the cable. It will take too long to unloose it. Cut it. It is a small loss anyway. You must come to Christ just as you are." And so, just as she was, she came and found the "peace that passeth all understanding," enabling her to bear her illness with bravery.

Twelve years later, while everyone about her was busy preparing for a bazaar, she was burdened with the thought that as an invalid she was utterly useless herself, and brooded over this through the long hours of the night. But the next day her faith prevailed; and, remembering the words of Dr. Milan which brought about her conversion, she took her pen and wrote the wonderful hymn, beginning, "Just as I am, without one plea." Later in the day Mrs. H. V. Elliott entered the room to tell her how the bazaar was progressing, and while there she read the hymn and took a copy of it. The great hymn was thus given to the world; and out of her helplessness Charlotte Elliott wrought a blessing to many souls that have been guided into salvation and wonderfully strengthened by her hymn.

13. "Almost Persuaded," Now to Believe

PHILIP BLISS,[1] 1838-1876

IN the year A. D. 62 a certain Roman citizen was cast into prison because of a multitude of accusations against him. At his hearing before Festus he appealed to Cæsar for justice, and was held for trial at Rome. Shortly afterward he was asked to state his defense before King Agrippa and Bernice, who were then visiting Festus. That defense, uttered by Paul—for he was the accused prisoner—is found in the twenty-sixth chapter of the Acts of the Apostles, and is one of the greatest addresses to be found in the Holy Scriptures. At the conclusion King Agrippa said to Paul: "Almost thou persuadest me to be a Christian," to which Paul replied, "I would to God that not only thou, but also all that hear me this day, were both almost and altogether such as I am, except these bonds."

A clergyman by the name of Brundage was once preaching upon this subject and concluded his sermon with these solemn words:

"He who is almost persuaded is almost saved, but to be almost saved is to be entirely lost." Philip Bliss was present and was so deeply impressed by these words that he wrote one of his most helpful hymns, based on the phrase "almost persuaded," as a direct result of this sermon. During the Moody revivals many souls, almost persuaded, were helped by the appeal of this hymn to decide for Christ before it was too late.

[1] The name, Philip P. Bliss, is often attached to his hymns, although the middle initial was an interpolation in his real name.

14. The Whole World Was Lost in the Darkness of Sin

PHILIP BLISS, 1838-1876

DR. S. EARL TAYLOR, formerly missionary secretary of the Methodist Episcopal Church, has visited Christian missions around the world, and has had unusual opportunity to hear missionary hymns sung in many different lands. But rarely has he ever been so thrilled by hymn-singing, he declares, as during an eclipse of the sun in the Orient. In India the natives have a superstitious dread of an eclipse of the sun. They fear that the sun is being swallowed by a demon of some sort.

Once Dr. Taylor was in Calcutta during an eclipse of the sun. For days before that event he saw the city's streets crowded with pilgrims on their way to various sacred places, where they hoped to worship and bathe in the Hooghly River just below the Ganges during the time of the eclipse, expecting thereby to ward off evil. When at last the fateful hour of darkness arrived hundreds of thousands of natives thronged the sacred waters, terrorized by the eclipse and making a great clamor because they feared that a great power of evil in the form of a snake was about to swallow the sun-god. As Dr. Taylor, looking from the Y. M. C. A. Building, witnessed this terrible evidence of heathenish superstition, he heard a group of native Christians singing in their meeting:

> The whole world was lost in the darkness of sin;
> The Light of the world is Jesus.

The effect was thrilling! For India's spiritual darkness is due solely to the eclipse of Jesus, the Light of the world, made by heathenism in the hearts of her benighted millions.

15. Blest Be the Tie That Binds

JOHN FAWCETT, 1739-1817

THE Rev. Dr. John Fawcett, pastor of the Baptist church in Wainsgate, Yorkshire, had accepted a call to a London church and had preached his farewell sermon, when the tender devotion of his parishioners compelled him to sacrifice his larger ambitions for a career in London, and he remained with them until his death. As a result of this experience he wrote the hymn, "Blest Be the Tie That Binds."

A young man was once the teacher of a class of unruly girls in D. L. Moody's Sunday school. One day he tottered into Mr. Moody's store, pale and bloodless, and exclaimed: "I have been bleeding at the lungs, and they have given me up to die. I must go away at once." "But you are not afraid to die?" asked Mr. Moody. "No," he replied, "but I must soon stand before God and give an account of my stewardship, and not one of my Sunday school scholars has been brought to Christ."

Immediately he called in all the scholars, appealing to them to accept Christ; and for ten days he worked and prayed with them as never before until each member of the class was saved. On the night when he left for the distant place, where he finally died, says Mr. Moody, "we held a true love feast. It was the very gate of heaven—that meeting." He prayed and they prayed, and then with streaming eyes they sang:

> "Blest be the tie that binds
> Our hearts in Christian love;
> The fellowship of kindred minds
> Is like to that above."

Bidding each farewell at the train, the dying man whispered that he would meet them all in heaven.

16. Be Not Dismayed Whate'er Betide

C. D. MARTIN

A BLIND man was seen crossing the street at a dangerous place in the Bronx, New York city. A friend nearby overheard him singing softly, "God will take care of you," and asked, "Why are you singing that hymn?" He replied: "Because I must cross this dangerous street, and maybe one of the many wagons might strike me and I might get killed. But the thought came to me that, even if it did occur, my soul would go straight to God. And if He led me across all right, it would be just another evidence of His care of me. So I could not help singing to myself, 'God will take care of you.' Hallelujah!"

A little Sunday school girl once told her mother she was never afraid to pass through a certain dark hallway leading to their home, "because," she explained, "I simply sing, 'God will take care of you,' and I always come through safely."

This hymn was sung at each session of the State Christian Endeavor Convention, Altoona, Pennsylvania, in 1910. At the close of one of the sessions a man, touched by the song, inquired after salvation. A little later some delegates, while singing this song at their hotel, noticed several men at the door of a nearby barroom attracted by the singing. One had a glass of beer in his hand, which he quietly poured into the gutter leading to the street before the strains of the song were finished.

17. O Beautiful for Spacious Skies

KATHARINE LEE BATES, 1859-

MISS KATHARINE LEE BATES, professor of English Literature in Wellesley College, is the author of this hymn. She wrote it in 1893 while on a Western tour that brought her first to the Columbian Exposition in Chicago. The patriotic impressions made upon her mind by the wonderful White City she bore westward with her as she journeyed to Colorado; and when at last she stood on the summit of Pike's Peak and beheld the far-spreading panorama below and the spacious skies above, her soul was stirred by the thought of the greatness and the God-given destiny of America. These lines were set ringing in her heart, and into a noble poem she has woven the beauties of that mountain-top vision:

> O beautiful for spacious skies,
> For amber waves of grain,
> For purple mountain majesties
> Above the fruited plain!

Each verse is rounded with a prayer that to the physical beauty of her native land God may add the highest moral beauty:

> America! America!
> God shed His grace on thee,
> And crown thy good with brotherhood
> From sea to shining sea!

Horatio Parker, one of the greatest of American composers, wrote a rich melody, "America the Beautiful," to which this hymn is set; though it is frequently sung, and most effectively, to the tune "Materna."

18. Fling Out the Banner: Let It Float

GEORGE WASHINGTON DOANE, 1799-1859

GEORGE WASHINGTON DOANE, once Protestant Episcopal Bishop of New Jersey, was born the same year in which General George Washington died—1799. His life, which spanned the years until 1859, was filled with remarkable activity. He graduated at Union College in 1818, began his ministry at Trinity Church, New York, was a professor in Trinity College, Hartford, Connecticut, and later rector of Trinity Church, Boston, when he was elected to be Bishop of New Jersey.

Five years after he became bishop, he founded on the banks of the Delaware River at Burlington, New Jersey, a Protestant Episcopalian school for girls, known as Saint Mary's Hall, about which the best traditions of the Diocese of New Jersey have centered. The Bishop took the liveliest interest in the school, and watched over the destiny of his educational child with fatherly anxiety.

His successor, Bishop John Scarborough, who inherited through his office this interest in the school, once told the writer how Bishop Doane came to write the famous missionary hymn, "Fling Out the Banner!" In 1848 there was to be a flag-raising at Saint Mary's Hall, and the girls of the school appealed to Bishop Doane to write a song for them to sing on that occasion. The result was the writing of this hymn, which was sung for the first time by the young ladies of the seminary, and has been sung at thousands of missionary meetings since then, to the spiritual stimulation of many souls.

19. Glory Be to the Father

ONE of the most universally accepted forms of worship among Protestants, who would praise the Triune God in song, is the ancient "Gloria Patri." This is, strictly within the meaning of the term, a doxology, for a doxology is an alleluia or other expression of praise to the Three Persons of the Holy Trinity. "Glory be to the Father, and to the Son, and to the Holy Ghost" expresses the fundamental doctrine of the Apostles' Creed, and at the same time utters worshipful praise to God.

The story of the exact origin of the "Gloria Patri" is not known, though it is thought by many hymnologists to have come to us from the apostolic age. The coming of Christ as a babe in Bethlehem was heralded by a hymn of the angels in the first Christmas gloria: "Glory to God in the highest, and on earth peace, good will toward men." After the Last Supper with the Saviour the apostles sang a hymn and went out, as it is recorded in the gospel. Hymn-singing was one of the peculiar customs of the early Christians observed by secular writers of that age. There is inspiration to us in the thought that the Christians of this day make such frequent use of the hymn to the Trinity, sung by Christians in the apostolic age.

It is said that on May 26, A. D. 735, when his death was approaching, The Venerable Bede, the most eminent sacred scholar of his age, asked his friends to carry him to that part of the room where he usually prayed; and there he sang the "Gloria Patri"; and when at last he had sung, "World without end, Amen," his spirit fled to the land of eternal life.

20. I Was a Wandering Sheep

HORATIUS BONAR, 1808-1889

THE Rev. Dr. Horatius Bonar, a graduate of the University of Edinburgh, was one of the founders of the Free Church of Scotland in 1843. He wrote a great many hymns that are widely used. In his hymn, "I Was a Wandering Sheep," he has told the story of salvation in simple terms that a child can understand.

Dr. Long has written an account of the revival in a girls' school in Massachusetts, where many of the girls had shown a great indifference to religion. Among the girls who laughed at the meetings and their results was one by the name of Helen B——. They sought to interest her in attending the prayer meetings, but all they could do was to pray for her. One evening, however, they were amazed to see Helen enter the meeting with eyes downcast and face very pale. After a few hymns and prayers each one quoted some favorite hymn verses. When Helen's turn came there was a silence, and then she began:

> "I was a wandering sheep,
> I did not love the fold."

"Her voice was low but distinct; and every word, as she uttered it, thrilled the hearts of the listeners. She repeated one stanza after another of that beautiful hymn of Bonar's, and not an eye, save her own, was dry, as with sweet emphasis she pronounced the last lines:

> 'No more a wayward child,
> I seek no more to roam.'

That single hymn told all. The wandering sheep, the wayward child, had returned."

26

21. Come, O Thou All-Victorious Lord

CHARLES WESLEY, 1707-1788

IN June, 1746, Charles Wesley visited Portland and preached to the workingmen who were employed in the quarries of that region; but he was evidently impressed that the hearts of some of his hearers were as hard as the stone in which they wrought day after day. This hymn is entitled: "Written Before Preaching at Portland," and perhaps the thoughts which inspired it can best be presented by quoting from his diary:

June 6. "I preached to a houseful of staring, loving people, from Jer. 50. 20. Some wept, but some looked quite unawakened. At noon and night I preached on the hill in the midst of the island. Most of the inhabitants came to hear, but few as yet feel the burden of sin, or the want of a Saviour.

"Sun., June 8.—After evening service we had all the islanders that were able to come. I asked, 'Is it nothing to you, all ye that pass by?' About half a dozen answered, 'It is nothing to us,' by turning their backs, but the rest hearkened with greater signs of emotion than I had before observed. I found faith at this time that our labors would not be in vain." The next day "the power and blessing came. My mouth and their hearts were opened. The rocks were broken in pieces, and melted into tears on every side. I continued exhorting them from seven till ten, to save themselves from this untoward generation. We could hardly part."

Wesley's hymn speaks in terms of the quarry-man's daily work:

> Come, O Thou all-victorious Lord,
> Thy power to us make known;
> Strike with the hammer of Thy word,
> And break these hearts of stone.

22. Saviour, Breathe an Evening Blessing

JAMES EDMESTON, 1791-1867

By profession an architect and surveyor, James Edmeston became eminent in this field. Sir G. Gilbert Scott, the noted architect, was one of his pupils. But Edmeston is remembered to-day chiefly by the hymns which he wrote. He was the author of over two thousand, most of them having been written for children. The most popular of them all is "Saviour, Breathe an Evening Blessing."

One evening in 1819 he was reading of Salte's exciting adventures, in a book entitled *Travels in Abyssinia,* when he came upon this passage concerning the natives, which was in striking contrast with what had gone before: "At night their short evening hymn, 'Jesu Mahaxaroo'—'Jesus, forgive us'— stole through the camp."

Its simple beauty and significance struck him so forcefully that he at once laid aside the fascinating book of travel and proceeded to compose the hymn,

> Saviour, breathe an evening blessing,
>   Ere repose our spirits seal;
> Sin and want we come confessing:
>   Thou canst save and Thou canst heal.

The hymn was sung at the close of evening worship at the church, which the author attended, in Homerton; and the beautiful custom was continued thereafter for many years. It was first published in *Sacred Lyrics* the year after it was written. Bishop Bickersteth afterward used the hymn in his *Christian Psalmody,* and in a later hymn book added another verse of his own composition, beginning: "Father, to Thy holy keeping." The line, "Should swift death this night o'ertake us," has been altered in some hymn books to read, "Be Thou nigh, should death o'ertake us," thus eliminating the reference to sudden death.

23. There's a Friend for Little Children

ALBERT MIDLANE, 1825-1909

WHAT responsibilities and opportunities are in the hands of a Sunday school teacher! Albert Midlane, an ironmonger, who wrote hundreds of Christian hymns, a large number of which have passed into common use, gave to his faithful teacher in the Sunday school at Newport, Isle of Wight, where he was born, the credit for starting him upon his poetic career as a little boy, as well as for shaping the thoughts and purposes of his early life. This teacher was a constant reader of poetry, and so lovingly guided his appreciation and his efforts in this field that before he was nine years old he wrote a series of verses that were greatly admired in his circle of older acquaintances.

Another influence had its bearing upon his life. His father died three months before he was born, and years later his mother said to him: "Albert, they told me when your dear father died that my child would be the Lord's gift to cheer and help me in my widowhood." This awakened in his heart a new sense of love for that divine "Friend for little children," whose everlasting and unchanging friendship is so tenderly acknowledged in this hymn.

Of all of his hymns this has proved to be the most popular. It was first scribbled in a little notebook which the author carried about with him. He said afterwards that it came straight from his heart. And it has reached the hearts of thousands of little children. When in his old age he was reduced to poverty, a popular subscription was taken among the children of England and a goodly sum was given to him as a token of their affection.

24. I'm But a Stranger Here

THOMAS RAWSON TAYLOR, 1807-1835

BORN at Ossett in Yorkshire, England, young Taylor received his earlier education at the Free School, Bradford, and at Leaf Square Academy, Manchester. At the age of fifteen he entered a merchant's office and later a printing establishment, where he worked until he was eighteen. His religious experience was so vital that he decided to leave business and enter the Christian ministry. To that end he matriculated at Airedale Independent College to prepare himself for ordination in the Congregational Church.

We are told that his health during college days was so precarious that he realized that he must be up and about his Master's business, as his time for witnessing to the truth might prove to be short. Accordingly, while pursuing his studies, he frequently preached the gospel in his college town and in the neighboring towns and villages. He was developing early that sense of other-worldliness that finds expression in his hymn.

At length he left college to be ordained, and in July, 1830, began serving the Howard Street Chapel in Sheffield. But this proved to be his only pastorate, and he had been there but six months when his health broke down and in January, 1831, he relinquished the charge. Shortly afterward he began teaching as a tutor in the classics at Airedale College, but after a time this too proved too much for his feeble body and he was obliged to resign. As night was closing about his life he wrote these lines,

> I'm but a stranger here,
> Heaven is my home.

He died in 1835. The words which he uttered in the sermon on the night before he died inspired Montgomery's hymn, "Servant of God, Well Done!" (*q. v.*, page 33).

25. From Every Stormy Wind That Blows

HUGH STOWELL, 1799-1865

CANON STOWELL, of Chester Cathedral, had little sympathy with the Tractarian Movement in the church, was thoroughly evangelical, and above all was a man of great power in prayer. When he was rector of Christ Church, Salford, such great crowds came to hear him preach that a magnificent new church had to be built to accommodate his audiences. Three years before going to Salford, desiring to give poetic expression to his faith and his comfort in prayer, he wrote this poem, entitled, "Peace at the Mercy Seat," which was first published in an illustrated annual, The Winter's Wreath, in 1828. It was but one of many poems with which he enriched Christian hymnody.

It has been sung through the decades by Christian people amidst varying degrees of trial and difficulty, bringing to their hearts the comforting thought of "a calm, a sure retreat" to be found at the "blood-bought mercy seat." But never has it been sung with more dramatic meaning than when in 1857 the eight American missionaries, the Rev. Albert Johnson, John E. Freeman, David E. Campbell, John McMullen and their wives sang it in Cawnpore, India, just before they and the two Campbell children suffered the death of Christian martyrs by order of the blood-thirsty Nana Sahib.

Stowell's son once wrote that his father's death illustrated Montgomery's lines,

> His watchword at the gates of death,
> He enters heaven by prayer.

"My father's last utterances," he added, "abundantly showed his love of and delight in prayer. Almost every word was prayer. . . . The morning of his death the only articulate words that we could catch, uttered two or three hours before his decease, were, 'Amen! Amen!'"

26. Our Thought of Thee Is Glad With Hope

JOHN GREENLEAF WHITTIER, 1807-1892

CONCORD, Massachusetts, is not only one of America's most sacred literary shrines, the old home of Emerson, Hawthorne, Thoreau, Alcott, Margaret Fuller, and Ellery Channing, but it is also a place of dramatic significance in the early struggle of the American colonists for freedom, the spot where in 1775

> Th' embattled farmers stood,
> And fired the shot heard round the world.

To this town of hallowed memories, just two years before his death, the Quaker poet, John G. Whittier, was invited by Daniel Lothrop, the publisher, and his wife. The occasion was a reception to be given in honor of the wife of General John A. Logan, who had distinguished himself in the Civil War and later in civic life.

At that time, however, Whittier, who was eighty-three years old and was suffering from the infirmities of advanced age, could only send this note of regret:

"I cannot be with you on the 14th, owing to the state of my health; but I send you some lines which I hope may not seem inappropriate. I am very truly thy friend, John G. Whittier."

Accompanying the letter, came a poem, entitled, "Our Country," and beginning with the lines,

> Our thought of thee is glad with hope,
> Dear country of our love and prayer.

Giving to God's grace devout acknowledgment for America's salvation when "tried as by furnace fires," his lines bear a special message to our own age:

> With peace that comes of purity,
> And strength to simple justice due,
> So runs our loyal dream of thee.
> God of our fathers! make it true.

27. Servant of God, Well Done!

JAMES MONTGOMERY, 1771-1854

THE Rev. Thomas Taylor, a Methodist minister, on the evening of October 14, 1816, was preaching a sermon, and in the course of his address he stated his hope that when he died he would die as an old soldier of Jesus Christ with his sword in his hand. The very next morning his family found him dead in his bed. The news of his sudden death was a shock to the wide circle of his friends, and among them was counted James Montgomery, the editor of *The Sheffield Iris,* who was already known as a great hymn writer.

In commemoration of Taylor's death and with the courageous words of his last sermon in mind, Montgomery wrote this hymn entitled "The Christian Soldier," which begins with these lines:

> "Servant of God, well done!
>   Rest from thy loved employ;
> The battle fought, the victory won,
>   Enter thy Master's joy."
> The voice at midnight came;
>   He started up to hear;
> A mortal arrow pierced his frame;
>   He fell; but felt no fear.

The hymn is not to be confused with another hymn with the same first line by Charles Wesley,

> Servant of God, well done!
>   Thy glorious warfare's past.

This latter appeared at the end of the published sermon by John Wesley, preached in the Tabernacle at Tottenham Court Row at the funeral of George Whitefield, who died September 30, 1770.

28. God of Our Fathers, Known of Old

RUDYARD KIPLING, 1865-

THOUGH never appointed poet laureate of England, the great British poet, Kipling, born in Bombay, India, has written more virile and enduring poetry than many another poet who has obtained that office as a mark of regal favor. When after a half century upon the British throne Queen Victoria celebrated her Diamond Jubilee, and "the captains and the kings" of earth assembled to do honor to the ruler who claimed "dominion over palm and pine," London witnessed the greatest pageant and the most elaborate ceremonies of the kind ever performed. And there arose a chorus of poetry from many bards in honor of that unusual event. But no note was sounded, combining such literary beauty and moral strength in its utterance, as that of "The Recessional."

Kipling's own account of the writing of the poem has been quoted by Dr. Wilbur F. Tillett:

"That poem gave me more trouble than anything I ever wrote. I had promised the Times a poem on the Jubilee, and when it became due I had written nothing that had satisfied me. The Times began to want that poem badly, and sent letter after letter asking for it. I made many more attempts, but no further progress. Finally the Times began sending telegrams. So I shut myself in a room with the determination to stay there until I had written a Jubilee poem. Sitting down with all my previous attempts before me, I searched through those dozens of sketches till at last I found just one line I liked. That was 'Lest we forget.' Round these words 'The Recessional' was written."

The first hymn book which included it as a hymn was the Baptist *Sursum Corda,* published in Philadelphia in 1898. Since that time it has passed into common use as a hymn of peace and patriotism.

29. My Lord, How Full of Sweet Content

MADAME GUYON (Jeanne Marie Bouvières de la Mothe),
1648-1717
(Translated by William Cowper, 1731-1800)

MADAME GUYON was a Mystic, a friend of the
great Fénelon, and an enthusiastic apostle of Quietism. Educated in a convent at Montargis, France,
the town in which she was born, she devoted much
study to the writings of Saint Francis de Sales,
Madame de Chantal, and Thomas à Kempis, which
largely determined the character of her faith. Her
marriage at the age of sixteen to the wealthy M.
Guyon resulted unhappily. After a series of long
illnesses he died in 1676.

Shortly afterward she started her career as an
evangelist of Quietism, and as the influence of her
teachings expanded she incurred the displeasure of
the Roman Catholic Church and a virulent persecution against her was begun. In 1686, when she came
to Paris, she was imprisoned in the Convent of Saint
Marie for eight months. Again after an ecclesiastical commission had warned her to be less active,
she was cast into prison at Vincennes in 1695 until
the following year. Refusing to cease her propa-
ganda, she was incarcerated in the Bastille from
1698 until 1702, expecting almost daily to be ex-
ecuted for heresy. After her release she was banished to a distant province, where she remained in
retirement with her daughter.

And yet in what spirit she bore these tribulations
for the sake of the faith that was within her we may
understand from William Cowper's translation of
her French hymn:

> My Lord, how full of sweet content
> I pass my years of banishment.
> Where'er I dwell, I dwell with Thee,
> In heaven or earth or on the sea.

30. Jesus, Where'er Thy People Meet

WILLIAM COWPER, 1731-1800

JOHN NEWTON and William Cowper were associated together in the preparation of *Olney Hymns,* which was published in 1779, not only to promote the faith and comfort of sincere Christians, but also, as Newton says in the Preface, "to perpetuate the remembrance of an intimate and endeared friendship" between these two devout men. Both of them were excellent hymn writers. Newton was ordained to the curacy of Olney in 1764. Cowper went to live in Olney in 1768. Among the many bonds which strengthened this mutual friendship was their common interest in a neighborhood prayer meeting.

The following year, 1769, the prayer meeting was removed to the great room in the Great House near the church. Newton said of it in a letter to Mr. Clunie, that April: "It is a noble place, with a parlor behind it, and holds one hundred and thirty people conveniently. Pray for us, that the Lord may be in the midst of us there, and that as He has now given us a Rehoboth, and has made room for us, so that He may be pleased to add to our numbers, and make us fruitful in the land."

To signalize the removal of the prayer meeting, each of them wrote a hymn for the collection of *Olney Hymns.* Newton's was "O Lord, Our Languid Frames Inspire," or, as it is better known, "Dear Shepherd of Thy People, Hear." Cowper's hymn was "Jesus, Where'er Thy People Meet," entitled, "On Opening a Place for Social Prayer." Cowper sometimes led these meetings; and the Rev. William Bull, of Newport Pagnell, who occasionally attended them, has recorded the opinion that some of those present "never heard praying that equaled Mr. Cowper's."

31. Jesus, Lover of My Soul

CHARLES WESLEY, 1707-1788

IN the Civil War of the sixties many drummer-boys had left school to join the army. One of them, named Tom, was called "the young deacon," as he was a great favorite and was respected by the soldiers for his religious life. Both his widowed mother and his sister were dead, so he had gone to war. One day he told the chaplain he had had a dream the night before. In his sleep he was greeted home again by his mother and little sister. "How glad they were!" he said. "My mother pressed me to her heart. I didn't seem to remember they were dead. O, sir, it was just as real as you are real now!" "Thank God, Tom," replied the chaplain, "that you have such a mother, not really dead but in heaven, and that you are hoping through Christ to meet her again."

The following day in frightful battle both armies swept over the same ground four times, and at night between the two armies lay many dead and wounded that neither dared approach. Tom was missing; but when the battle roar was over they recognized his voice singing, softly and beautifully, "Jesus, Lover of My Soul." When he had sung,

> "Leave, ah! leave me not alone,
> Still support and comfort me,"

the voice stopped and there was silence. In the morning the soldiers found Tom sitting on the ground and leaning against a stump—dead. But they knew that his "helpless soul" had found refuge with Jesus, the Lover of the soul.

37

32. When I Survey the Wondrous Cross

ISAAC WATTS, 1674-1748

MATTHEW ARNOLD declared the greatest Christian hymn in the English language to be "When I Survey the Wondrous Cross." At least it is admittedly the greatest hymn of a great hymn-writer, Isaac Watts, the father of modern English hymnody. He was the son of a deacon in the Independent Church, who had no sympathy with young Watts's custom of making rhymes and verses when a boy. At the age of eighteen Watts was one day ridiculing some of the poor hymns then sung in the churches, when his father said to him, sarcastically, "Make some yourself, then." Accordingly, Watts set himself to writing a hymn, and produced the lines beginning: "Behold the glories of the Lamb." That was the start of his eminent career as a hymn-writer.

He became a clergyman, but illness compelled him to give up the pastorate, and for thirty-six years he remained at the home of Sir Thomas Abbey at Theobaldo, continuing his hymn-writing, which had reached its highest expression in this hymn, based on Paul's words, "God forbid that I should glory, save in the cross of our Lord Jesus Christ."

Once, after this hymn had been sung in the Church of Saint Edmund, London, Father Ignatius repeated to his congregation the last two lines of the hymn impressively—

> "Love so amazing, so divine,
>   Demands my soul, my life, my all."

And he added: "Well, I am surprised to hear you sing that. Do you know that altogether you put only fifteen shillings in the collection bag this morning?"

33. All Glory, Laud, and Honor

SAINT THEODULPH, ?-821

SOME of our best hymns were originally written many centuries ago in the Latin language, and have been brought into our English hymnody by devout modern translators. In the year A. D. 820 Theodulph, the Bishop of Orleans, was imprisoned at Metz by King Louis, the Debonnaire, who was the son of Charlemagne. The Bishop had been falsely accused of disloyalty to his king, but he bore with patience his captivity and the ignominy brought upon him by suspicious gossipers.

While in prison his meditations were upon the King of kings, and, taking the beautiful story of Christ's triumphal entry into Jerusalem as his theme, he wrote a Palm Sunday hymn that has survived to the Christian Church these eleven hundred years:

All glory, laud and honor to Thee, Redeemer, King,
To whom the lips of children made sweet hosannas ring.

Our translation was made by the Rev. Dr. John Mason Neale.

An ancient tradition has it that the Bishop trained a chorus within the cloisters to sing his hymn with beautiful effect; and once they were singing it thus while King Louis and his court were passing on their way to the Cathedral. So enchanted was the king by its beauty that he commanded that the Bishop be released from his prison at once. The following year he died; but his church canonized him because of his preeminent piety. And to-day he is known as "Saint Theodulph."

34. The Day of Resurrection

JOHN OF DAMASCUS, ?-780

EASTERTIDE brings a worldwide joy, and its coming is celebrated in many different ways. Dean Stanley once penned a description of an Easter celebration in the Greek Church in which the hymn, "The Day of Resurrection," was sung in the original Greek, as it was first written, and with all of its original beauty:

"As midnight approached, the Archbishop with his priests, accompanied by the king and queen, left the church and stationed themselves on the platform, which was raised considerably from the ground, so that they were distinctly seen by the people. . . . Suddenly a single report from a cannon announced that twelve o'clock had struck, and that Easter Day had begun. Then the old Archbishop elevated the cross, exclaimed in a loud, exalted tone: '*Christos anesti.*' And instantly every single individual of all that host took up the cry, . . . with a shout, 'Christ is risen! Christ is risen!'

"At the same moment the impressive darkness was succeeded by a blaze of light from thousands of tapers. . . . Everywhere men clasped each other's hands and congratulated one another and embraced with countenances beaming with delight, as though to each one separately some wonderful happiness had been proclaimed; and so in truth it was. And all the while, rising above the mingling of many sounds, each one of which was a sound of gladness, the aged priests were distinctly heard chanting forth this glorious old 'hymn of victory' in tones so loud and clear that they seemed to have regained their youth to tell the world that Christ is risen from the dead."

35. All Hail the Power of Jesus' Name:

EDWARD PERRONET, 1726-1792

THE Rev. Edward Perronet was a most devout man, who had the courage of his convictions and was not afraid to suffer for what he thought to be right. He lived in the days of the Wesleys and was intimate with them, and the philanthropic Lady Huntingdon was his patroness for a time. But these friends he felt it necessary to surrender because he conscientiously differed with them on some points of belief. His immortal hymn, "All Hail the Power of Jesus' Name," has proved a blessing to Protestants of all beliefs.

One of the most dramatic instances of its use was found in the experience of the Rev. E. P. Scott in India. His friends had urged him not to venture near a certain barbarous inland tribe, whom he wished to evangelize. But he went forward with high courage, never wavering in his duty, and trusting in God to protect him. When at last he reached their country among the hills, he came upon a company of these savages. Immediately they surrounded him, pointing their spears at him with threatening scowls. He had nothing in his hands but his violin; and so, closing his eyes, he began to play and sing, "All Hail the Power of Jesus' Name." When at last he opened his eyes he expected to be killed instantly. But his life had been spared through the singing of the hymn. Their spears had dropped, and they received him first with curiosity and interest, and then later with eagerness, as he told them the gospel story and won their hearts to the will of Jesus Christ.

36. Stand Up, Stand Up for Jesus:

GEORGE DUFFIELD, JR., 1818-1888

THE hymn, "Stand Up, Stand Up for Jesus," was
written during the great revival of 1858, that came
to be known as "The Work of God in Philadelphia."
It was based upon the dying words of the Rev.
Dudley A. Tyng, one of the most active ministers
in the revival. It is said that, when he preached
on March 30, 1858, at the noonday prayer meeting
in Jayne's Hall, five thousand men listened to his
sermon from the text, "Go now, ye that are men,
and serve the Lord," and that before the close of
the meeting over a thousand expressed their purpose
to become Christians.

A few days later at "Brookfield," not far from
Conshohocken, Pennsylvania, he left his study for
a moment and went out to the barn, where a mule
was working, harnessed to a machine, shelling corn.
When he patted the mule on the head, his sleeve
caught in the cogs of the wheel and his arm was
frightfully torn.

After a painful but short illness, death finally
claimed him. As he was dying, his father asked
him if he had any message for his fellow ministers
in the revival. He replied, "Let us all stand up for
Jesus." That message was borne to them along with
the sorrowful news of his death. Dr. George
Duffield, Jr., the following Sunday preached a memorial sermon on his late friend, Tyng, taking as his
text Ephesians 6. 14; and he wrote this hymn, based
upon Tyng's dying words, as a fitting climax to the
thought of his sermon. A reference to the text of
Dudley Tyng's memorable sermon to the men in
Jayne's Hall is to be found in the line,

Ye that are men now serve Him.

37. From Greenland's Icy Mountains

REGINALD HEBER, 1783-1826

BISHOP REGINALD HEBER, after years of longing for the spread of the gospel in India, crowned his career with a few years of most useful service as Bishop of Calcutta. He made extensive visitations among the struggling missions nearly a century ago and ordained the first Christian native, Christian David. At last he laid down his life, a victim of fever, as a result of his labors in that benighted land.

During the years of his life as rector of Hodnet, while longing for a career in India, he wrote many hymns, as well as other forms of literary productions, and won the respect and friendship of Milman, Southey, and other littérateurs.

One Saturday afternoon, the day before Whitsunday, 1819, he was at Wrexham Vicarage with his father-in-law, Dr. Shipley, Dean of Saint Asaph. Dr. Shipley was planning to preach on the following morning a sermon in aid of the Society for the Propagation of the Gospel in Foreign Parts, and in the evening Reginald Heber was to begin a series of lectures in the same church. As they sat together with some friends the Dean asked him to write a hymn on a missionary theme to be sung at the morning service. After Heber had retired for a while he returned and the Dean asked him: "What have you written?" Heber in reply read the first three verses of "From Greenland's Icy Mountains." The Dean exclaimed that they were very satisfactory. "No, no," replied Heber, "the sense is not complete." And so he added one more verse—"Waft, waft, ye winds, His story"—and the whole hymn was sung the next morning at the service.

38.   O Love That Wilt Not Let Me Go

GEORGE MATHESON, 1842-1906

DR. GEORGE MATHESON was one of the most beloved clergymen in the Church of Scotland. His
writings were numerous and of a high order. But
the marvel of it all is that he was able to accomplish so much without his sight; for from the age of
fifteen he was totally blind. His hymn, beginning,
"O Love that wilt not let me go," was sung out of
his blindness and gives evidence of the courage with
which he bore his great affliction.

His own story of how he came to write the hymn
is well worth quoting: "My hymn was composed in
the manse of Innellan on the evening of June 6,
1882. I was at the time alone. It was the day of
my sister's marriage, and the rest of the family
were staying overnight in Glasgow. Something had
happened to me, which was known only to myself;
and which caused the most severe mental suffering. It was the quickest bit of work I ever did in
my life. I had the impression rather of having it
dictated to me by some inward voice than of working it out myself."

William T. Stead quotes this letter from a cor-
respondent: "At a time of great spiritual darkness,
when God, Christ, and heaven seemed to have gone
out of my life, . . . I heard this hymn sung in a
little country chapel. The first two lines haunted
me for weeks, and at last brought light and comfort
to my dark soul."

39. Now Thank We All Our God

MARTIN RINKART, 1586-1649

THE Thirty Years' War in Germany from 1618 to 1648 devastated the land and inflicted incredible hardships on a long-suffering people. But the German Protestants remained true to their faith and bore their trials bravely for conscience' sake, at last winning honorable respite from their sufferings in the Peace of Westphalia, October 24, 1648.

Among the bravest of the sufferers from the war was the Rev. Martin Rinkart, who wrote the hymn originally in German, "Now Thank We All Our God." It is generally supposed that he wrote it as a *Te Deum* of praise because of the restoration of peace at the close of thirty years of horrible strife.

Catherine Winkworth, who translated this hymn into English, once wrote of him: "So great were Rinkart's own losses and charities that he had the utmost difficulty in finding bread and clothes for his children, and was forced to mortgage his future income for several years. Yet how little his spirit was broken by all these calamities is shown by this hymn and others that he wrote; some, indeed, speaking of his own country's sorrows, but all breathing the same spirit of unbounded trust and readiness to give thanks."

Rinkart was a skilled musician, as well as a poet; and, besides, he wrote seven dramas based upon the Restoration Period which were produced at the one hundredth anniversary of the Reformation. But he is best known to posterity through his hymns.

40. Golden Harps Are Sounding

FRANCES RIDLEY HAVERGAL, 1836-1879

MISS FRANCES RIDLEY HAVERGAL was the daughter of a clergyman of the Church of England, the Rev. W. H. Havergal. He was both musician and hymn-writer; and his gifted daughter, consecrating her life and her talents to the Master, wrote many helpful hymns, setting some of them to her own music, as is illustrated by the hymn, "Golden Harps Are Sounding."

Miss Anne Steele, who lived and wrote some of the best hymns in the eighteenth century, frequently signed her hymns with the name "Theodosia." Miss Havergal has been compared with Miss Steele, and is sometimes styled "the Theodosia of the nineteenth century," so influential has her life proved to be through her hymns as well as through her many other good works.

The Havergal manuscripts contain the following account of the writing of this hymn: "When visiting at Parry Barr," Miss Havergal "walked to the boys' schoolroom, and being very tired she leaned against the playground wall while Mr. Snepp went in. Returning in ten minutes, he found her scribbling on an old envelope. At his request she gave him the hymn just penciled, 'Golden harps are sounding.' Her popular tune, 'Hermas,' was composed for this hymn."

At the age of forty-two she died at Caswell Bay, Swansea. But shortly before she passed away, closing a life of rare usefulness in the salvation of many souls, she gathered up her strength and sang:

> "Golden harps are sounding
> Angel voices ring,
> Pearly gates are opened . . ."

41. Guide Me, O Thou Great Jehovah

WILLIAM WILLIAMS, 1717-1791

THE best known of the hymns by William Williams was originally written in the Welsh language and illustrates some of the characteristics of Welsh hymnody, which has been well compared in its simplicity and transparency to Hebrew poetry. In its emotional language and directness of appeal it relies more upon a simple expression of strong, spiritual feeling than upon the niceties of artistic law.

The author of this hymn came to be popularly known as "the Sweet Singer of Wales." Coming under the influence of Daniel Rowlands, a noted revivalist, he devoted his life to evangelism for which he was well fitted, for he was a remarkable singer and a powerful preacher. He became a deacon in the Church of England, but never took higher orders. His first hymn book, *Hallelujah,* was published in 1744, when he was but twenty-seven years old.

This hymn, which likens life's progress to the journey of Israel toward the Promised Land, was first translated into English by the Rev. Peter Williams. The first verse of this translation William Williams adopted, but translated two other verses himself, adding a fourth in English, "Musing on Thy habitation."

When Richard Knill, the missionary, lay dying he frequently sang this hymn, and its comforting assurance dispelled his "anxious fears." Toward the end he called his daughter and said: "I cannot sing. Sing for me my favorite hymn." She sang it to the tune, "Rousseau's Dream," and whenever she came to the last verse he would try his best to join in those lines, until at last he was borne "through the swelling current" and landed "safe on Canaan's shore."

47

42. Thy Life Was Given for Me

("I gave My life for thee")

FRANCES RIDLEY HAVERGAL, 1836-1879

THE first real hymn written by Miss Havergal was composed when she was but a month past her twenty-first birthday. On January 10, 1858, while visiting in Germany, she entered the study of a German minister. Quite tired, she sat down and her eyes lit upon an inscription, which had been placed under a picture of Jesus Christ: "I did this for thee: what hast thou done for Me?" As she gazed on the face of the suffering Redeemer the lines of the hymn framed themselves in her mind and, taking a pencil, she wrote them on the back of a circular. But when she read them over she felt that they expressed her emotions of that hour so inadequately that she exclaimed to herself: "This is not poetry. I will not go to the trouble to copy this"; and she crumpled up the circular and cast it into the fire.

But immediately something impelled her to rescue it, and she seized it, singed as it was by the flame, and a moment later placed it in her pocket.

A short time afterward she called upon an old woman in the almshouse. Miss Havergal tells us: "She began to talk to me, as she always did, about her dear Saviour, and I thought I would see if the simple old woman would care for these verses, which I felt sure nobody else would care to read. So I read them to her, and she was so delighted with them that when I went back I copied them out, and kept them, and now the hymn is more widely known than any."

Her father, the Rev. W. H. Havergal, ever since her mother died when Frances was eleven years old, had been her confidant and had encouraged the development of her talents. When she returned home one day she showed these verses to him. He was so delighted with them that he composed a tune, called

"Baca," for this hymn. It was published two years later in a leaflet. Originally her first line was, "I gave My life for thee." But when in 1871 it was included in *Church Hymns,* she was induced to change the line to its present form, "Thy life was given for me."

Years later she wrote: "I was so overwhelmed on Sunday at hearing three of my hymns touchingly sung in Perry Church. I never before realized the high privilege of writing for the 'great congregation,' especially when they sang 'I Gave My Life for Thee' to my father's tune, 'Baca.' "

43. Come Unto Me, Ye Weary

WILLIAM CHATTERTON DIX, 1837-1898

THE son of a surgeon in Bristol, England, the author of this hymn was educated in Bristol, but achieved his business success in Glasgow, Scotland. He was active, not only as a hymn-writer and a hymn-book editor, but also as an insurance man— an odd combination! Julian mentions twenty of his hymns which are in common use. None of them, however, is more tenderly beautiful than this hymn, which takes as its theme Christ's words, "Come unto Me all ye that labor and are heavy laden, and I will give you rest."

It was a pathetic coincidence when, in 1862, Doctor George Washington Bethune, a clergyman of the Dutch Reformed Church, died suddenly on the day after he wrote his famous hymn. "When Time Seems Short and Death Is Near." But it was probably more than a mere coincidence that the writing of this hymn,

> Come unto Me, ye weary,
> And I will give you rest,

was quickly followed by the recovery of Mr. Dix from an illness. He has told the story in his own words:

"I was ill and depressed at the time, and it was almost to idle away the hours that I wrote the hymn. I had been ill for many weeks, and felt weary and faint, and the hymn really expresses the languidness of body from which I was suffering at the time. Soon after its composition I recovered, and I always look back to that hymn as the turning point in my illness."

The hymn has brought comfort to many another weary soul, besides its author, with its cheering echo of the divine promise of rest from oppression, "Of pardon, grace, and peace."

44. Welcome, Happy Morning! Age to Age Shall Say

VENANTIUS HONORIUS CLEMENTIANUS FORTUNATUS, 530-609
(Translated by John Ellerton, 1826-1893)

THE author of the Latin hymn, "On the Resurrection of the Master," was once a student at Ravenna in his youth and became almost blind while pursuing his studies. Praying to God for recovery of his sight, he anointed his eyes with oil that had been brought to him from a lamp at Saint Martin's altar in Tours, and his sight was fully restored. In gratitude for what he regarded as a miracle, he made the long pilgrimage from Ravenna to Tours and worshiped at the shrine of Saint Martin. This led him to devote the rest of his life to France. At Poitiers he came under the beneficent influence of the pious Queen Rhadegunda, who induced him to become ordained, and after her death he was made Bishop of Poitiers.

The whole poem, from a part of which the English clergyman, the Rev. John Ellerton, translated this hymn, was one hundred and ten lines long and was dedicated to Bishop Felix of Nantes. It was but one of many poetical works which fell from his pen, among the best known being "The Royal Banners Forward Go," as translated by Doctor John Mason Neale. "Welcome, Happy Morning!" expresses eloquently the intense joy which Eastertime brings to every age. The line, "Tread the path of darkness," gives hint of the blindness of Fortunatus in his youth, while the last verse seems to sing of the miracle which released him from that darkness, "Bring again our daylight: day returns with Thee." Jerome of Prague suffered the death of martyrdom in being burned to death at the stake on May 30, 1416. As the flames rose about him he sang this ancient hymn. His last words were: "This soul in flames I offer, Lord, to Thee."

45. Shepherd of Tender Youth

CLEMENT OF ALEXANDRIA (circ. 170-220)
(Translated by Henry M. Dexter, 1821-1890)

To Titus Flavius Clemens, which, according to the ancient writer Eusebius, was the full name of Saint Clement, is attributed the authorship of the "Hymn of the Saviour," the oldest Christian hymn in existence. Born in Athens, he studied philosophy with the great teachers of many lands and became a Stoic and an Eclectic. In Alexandria he was converted to Christianity by the teaching of Pantænus, then at the head of the great Catechetical School. When Pantænus became a missionary Clement succeeded him as master of the school, 190-203 A. D.; and among those to whom he interpreted the divine "Shepherd of tender youth" were the famous Origen and Alexander, who was later Bishop of Jerusalem. In after years persecution drove him away from Alexandria and little is known of the rest of his life.

About the end of the second century he wrote this hymn in the Greek language, and in its original form it had wide use in the Eastern Church. The first line, literally translated, is: "Tamer of steeds unbridled"; but a New England Congregational clergyman, Doctor Henry M. Dexter, in 1848 softened this phrase into the line, "Shepherd of tender youth." The English translation of this hymn, first published in *The Congregationalist,* December 21, 1849, has found an important place among the Christian hymns of childhood in this country and in England. Doctor Dexter was pastor of a church in Manchester, New Hampshire, when he made the translation; in 1849 he served the Berkeley Street Church in Boston, and in 1867 became editor of *The Congregationalist.*

46. Flung to the Heedless Winds

MARTIN LUTHER, 1483-1546
(Translated by John Alexander Messenger, circ. 1840)

Two years after attending the Diet of Worms, 1521, "the point from which" (as Macaulay declares) "modern European history takes its rise," Martin Luther wrote his first hymn. He was then, 1523, engaged in writing a German translation of the Holy Bible. The manner in which he was being hounded, maligned, and persecuted by the Roman Catholic Church for his evangelical teaching and his utter contempt of ecclesiastical authority only stirred his independent soul to greater courage.

When, however, two monks, Heinrich Voes and Johann Esch of Antwerp, were tried for heresy in Cologne, and on June 30, 1523, were burned to death at the stake in Brussels, his heart broke forth into "A New Song of the Two Martyrs for Christ, burnt at Brussels by the Sophists of Louvain." From this John A. Messenger made the translation,

> Flung to the heedless winds,
>   Or on the waters cast,
> The martyrs' ashes, watched,
>   Shall gathered be at last.

It has been said that Luther had in mind also the martyrdom of John Huss, the great hero of the Czecho-Slovakians, who was persecuted for his faith by the Roman Catholic clergy and finally was cited before the Council of Constance and was burned at the stake in 1414. After his death his ashes and the earth on which they fell were cast upon the waters of the Rhine River. While he was being burned to death so great was his fortitude that he sang the "Kyrie Eleison,"—"Lord, have mercy upon us!"

1735-
1662

47. Behold the Saviour of Mankind

SAMUEL WESLEY, 1662-1735

THE Rev. Samuel Wesley, father of John and Charles Wesley, was Rector of Epworth, in England, for forty years until his death. In the Epworth Rectory were born both of his distinguished sons. In this home he suffered many trials and tribulations: his barn was blown down, the rectory was partly burned in 1703, miscreants by night burned his flax and at another time stabbed his three cows which helped to feed his numerous family; and he became seriously involved in debt as a result of these and other misfortunes. The crowning disaster was the complete destruction of the rectory by fire in 1709.

Two remarkable rescues, however, were made from the fire which yielded momentous results in after years. One was the saving of the six-year-old boy, John, who had been caught by the fire on the second floor. A parishioner by standing on the shoulders of another managed to reach the upper window, seized the frightened boy, and passed him to safety—that boy who was destined to be the founder of the great Wesleyan movement.

The other rescue was effected by a draft of wind that carried a piece of paper out of the window to a distant point in the rectory garden, where it was found after the fire—the manuscript of this hymn, written the day before, "Behold the Saviour of Mankind," by which chiefly Samuel Wesley is known to this generation as a hymn-writer. Charles Wesley on July 18, 1738, used the hymn as a means of bringing to salvation two criminals in Newgate Prison, condemned to die the very next day.

48. Onward, Christian Soldiers

SABINE BARING-GOULD, 1834-

IN Yorkshire, England, where Doctor Baring-Gould was stationed as curate of Horbury, it is the custom to observe Whitmonday as a day of festival for the school children. In 1865 his school was invited to march to a neighboring village, there to join the children of another school in the festival exercises. As he could not find a suitable hymn for the children to sing while marching from one village to another, he sat up late into the night to compose a hymn; and out of those midnight hours came the lines, "Onward, Christian soldiers," to which the children marched toward their festival and to which hundreds of thousands of Christians have marched in the decades since it was written.

> With the cross of Jesus
> Going on before

refers to the cross, borne at the head of the procession; while the many banners, following it, are pictured in the line, "See His banners go!"

It was published in the *Church Times* in 1865.

The hymn with its stirring tune, written later by Sir Arthur Sullivan, makes an ideal processional and has been widely used, not only in places of worship, but also upon a great variety of other occasions. Allan Sutherland, in *Famous Hymns of the World,* describes the wild rejoicing in Philadelphia on election night, 1905, when to signalize the victory of the Reform Movement thousands paraded the streets, singing this hymn; also its use in cheering Christian Japanese soldiers, starting for the war in 1904. It was the battle song of Roosevelt's Progressive campaign in 1912. In the World War it was a prime favorite, and was sung by General Feng Yü Hsiang's Eleventh Division of Chinese Christian soldiers as they advanced to battle before Peking in May, 1922.

49. Tell Me the Old, Old Story

KATHERINE HANKEY (1866)

"I LOVE to Tell the Story," and that other equally popular hymn by Miss Hankey, "Tell Me the Old, Old Story," are both centos taken from a long poem on the life of Christ, which was written in two parts. Miss Hankey, the daughter of a banker, was taken seriously ill in her home in England, and for a long time was confined to her bed. At last the malady subsided, and she entered upon an extended period of convalescence through the months of 1866.

Grateful to her Lord and Master for her recovery and for the story of salvation "that satisfies my longings," as she expressed it, she made the long days radiant with meditations on the life of Jesus; and out of these meditations wrote a long poem on the story of His life. The first part, which was begun in January, 1866, was entitled "The Story Wanted." The second part, which was completed in November of that same year, was in the nature of a sequel to the first part, as is implied by its title, "The Story Told."

It is said that the year after it was written, 1867, the composer, Doctor William H. Doane, was attending the International Convention of the Y. M. C. A. then being held in Montreal, and when Major General Russell read the lines, "Tell me the old, old story," Doane was so greatly moved that he secured a copy and afterward took it with him to the White Mountains, where he composed the winsome melody to which it is sung.

50. Jesus, Thy Blood and Righteousness

COUNT NICOLAUS LUDWIG VON ZINZENDORF, 1700-1760
(Translated by John Wesley, 1703-1791)

BOTH the writer and the translator of this hymn went to America as missionaries to the Indians in the early part of the eighteenth century, and both of them led religious movements which resulted in the establishment of great churches. John Wesley became the founder of Methodism. Count Zinzendorf is known as the second founder of the Moravian Brethren's Unity. To the Moravians, hitherto persecuted and exiled, he gave religious freedom and a hospice on his estate at Berthelsdorf in 1722. There under his guidance they reorganized their church, sent foreign missionaries to neglected heathen, and established communities in distant lands. One of these was the famous settlement at Bethlehem, Pennsylvania.

In 1739, when the Count was making a sea voyage from Saint Thomas, West Indies, he wrote this remarkable hymn. Although as a boy he was educated in pietistic teachings, he is said to have been converted by seeing the famous painting, "Ecce Homo," which hangs in the Düsseldorf Gallery and pictures the bowed head of Christ, crowned with thorns. Perhaps he still cherished in his memory that vision of the Man of Sorrows, when in this hymn he wrote of the "holy, meek, unspotted Lamb," "Who died for me, e'en me t' atone."

John Wesley owed much of spiritual inspiration to the doctrines and example of the Moravian Brethren, whom he first met in 1735 on his missionary voyage to America; and while he wrote few original English hymns, he turned to the Moravian hymns in German for a fitting expression of the doctrines he sought to emphasize, and translated them into English. This hymn was one of Wesley's first translations.

51. Mine Eyes Have Seen the Glory of the Coming of the Lord

JULIA WARD HOWE, 1819-1910

CHAPLAIN CHARLES C. McCABE, afterwards a bishop of the Methodist Episcopal Church, was confined in Libby Prison during a part of the Civil War. In his famous lecture on "The Bright Side of Life in Libby Prison," he used to tell this story of the arrival of the news from the Battle of Gettysburg:

"I had a relative in Richmond, a stanch rebel. The day they received the first tidings from Gettysburg he came to see me, his face wreathed in smiles: 'Have you heard the news?' 'What news?' 'Forty thousand Yankee prisoners on their way to Richmond!' I was astounded! In dumb amazement I listened to the Confederate officers speculating where the new prisoners should be stowed away, and how they were to be fed. I went upstairs and told the news. Despondency settled down into every heart.

"That night as we assembled for 'family prayers' and sang, as was always our wont the Long-meter Doxology, it trembled out from quavering voices up to Him who has said, 'Glorify Me in the fires.' I slept none that night, listening wearily to the watch calling the hours and singing out as he did so, 'All's well.' When the day broke I waited for the footsteps of 'Old Ben,' a character well known to every inmate of Libby. He was the prison news agent and sold papers at twenty-five cents apiece. At last his footfall came. He pushed the door ajar, looked around for a moment on the sleepers, and then raising his arms he shouted, 'Great news in de papers!'

"Did you ever see a resurrection? I never did but this once. O, how those men sprang to their feet! And what was the news? The telegraph operator at Martinsburg, when putting those ciphers to the four, had clicked the instrument once too often. There was a mistake of thirty-six thousand! More yet! Lee was driven back, the Potomac was swollen, the pontoons were washed away! I have stood by when friends long-parted meet again with raining tears and fond embrace, but never did I witness such joy as swept into those strong men's faces, where the deepest sorrow sat but a moment before. Well, what did we do? Why, we sang; sang as saved men do; sang till Captains Flynn and Sawyer, immured in the lowest dungeons below and doomed to die within ten days, heard us and wondered; sang till the very walls of Libby quivered in the melody as five hundred of us joined in the chorus of Mrs. Julia Ward Howe's 'Battle Hymn of the Republic,' 'Mine eyes have seen the glory of the coming of the Lord.' "

This hymn was written in 1861, at the beginning of the Civil war in the United States, inspired partly by the scene of troops hurrying from the North to Southern battlefields. All during that terrible struggle it was the great war song of the Union armies. During the recent World War it was sung by English-speaking troops from both sides of the Atlantic.

52. Jesus Shall Reign Where'er the Sun

ISAAC WATTS, 1674-1748

AMONG the many monuments of England's greatest heroes in Westminster Abbey, London, there stands a memorial tablet to Doctor Isaac Watts, upon which the poet is represented with pen in hand writing at a table, and above him an angel is whispering to him words of inspiration. Thus has England honored the memory of the father of modern English hymns.

His missionary hymn, beginning, "Jesus shall reign where'er the sun," has been used the world over on missionary occasions. It was originally entitled "Christ's Kingdom Among the Gentiles," and is part of his admirable translation of the second part of the seventy-second psalm.

Probably no instance of its use has been more dramatic than when it was sung in one of the South Sea Islands in 1862. The conversion of the South Sea Islanders from cannibalism to Christianity is one of the most brilliant pages in the history of missionary conquest. One of the tribal kings had been with many of his people converted to Christianity, and he decided to proclaim a Christian constitution for his government. Accordingly, he set apart a certain day for the final ceremony. Over five thousand natives of the islands of Tonga, Fiji, and Samoa were present, rescued from the savagery of heathenism; and during the ceremony they all united their voices in singing:

> "Jesus shall reign where'er the sun
> Does His successive journeys run."

53. Lead, Kindly Light, Amid th' Encircling Gloom

JOHN HENRY NEWMAN, 1801-1890

THIS prayer-hymn, cast in high poetic form, was penned by John Henry Newman, afterward a cardinal in the Roman Catholic Church, while on shipboard on Sunday, June 16, 1833. It is said that the ship had been compelled to proceed slowly because of the dense fog that encompassed it. Doctor Newman was returning to Marseilles, France, from a visit he had made to Italy. While in Sicily he was taken seriously ill and on his recovery he waited for his ship in Palermo for three weeks.

Probably both of these facts entered somewhat into the imagery of the hymn, as is evidenced by such phrases as "th' encircling gloom" and "The night is dark, and I am far from home."

The thought and sentiment of the hymn, however, were wrought out of the mental darkness in which Newman was then groping. Some time before, he wrote this note: "Now in my room in Oriel College, slowly advancing, etc., and led on by God's hand blindly, not knowing whither he is taking me." This darkness, beclouding his faith, had become still deeper during the summer of his Italian journey, during which he wrote "Lead, Kindly Light." But the expression of his supreme trust in God, which shines through these lines, so universally popular, has helped many a soul that has yearned for guidance "amid th' encircling gloom."

54. Gentle Jesus, Meek and Mild

CHARLES WESLEY, 1707-1788

JOHN B. GOUGH with a friend one day went up to a small garret room. A feeble voice said, "Come in!" and they entered. Through the gloom they saw a boy, ten years old, lying on a heap of chips. "What are you doing there?" they asked. "Hush!" he replied; "I am hiding." As he showed his bruised and swollen arms, he added: "Poor father got drunk and beat me because I would not steal. . . . Once I went to ragged school and they taught me 'Thou shalt not steal,' and told me about God in heaven. I will not steal, sir, if my father kills me."

The friend said: "I don't know what to do with you. Here's a shilling. I will see what we can do for you." The boy looked at it a minute, and then said: "But please, sir, wouldn't you like to hear my little hymn?" They marveled that a lad suffering from cold and hunger and bruises could sing a hymn; but they answered: "Yes, we will hear you." And then in a low, sweet voice he sang, "Gentle Jesus, meek and mild." At the conclusion he said: "That's my little hymn. Good-by."

Next morning they mounted the stairs again, knocking at the door, but there came no answer. They opened the door and went in. The shilling lay on the floor, and there too lay the boy—dead, but with a brave smile on his face. His "Gentle Jesus" had taken him home to heaven.

55. In the Cross of Christ I Glory

JOHN BOWRING, 1792-1872

AMONG the hymn-writers represented in our hymnals are to be found a shoemaker, a prisoner in bondage, an editor, several bishops and a cardinal, a converted slave-trader, a lawyer, a blind woman, a student, and a college professor. None, however, bore a greater distinction, or won higher fame in the public life of a statesman, than did Sir John Bowring. He represented the English government in France at one time. Later he was consul to Hongkong, and afterward governor of Hongkong. He became a great factor in the political development of the Orient. Twice he was a member of the British Parliament and was knighted in 1854. Besides his distinctions in statecraft, he won high literary honors and was the master of thirteen different languages, having made translations from all of them into English.

In spite of all these great earthly successes, and in spite of the fact that he was a Unitarian by faith, he humbled himself before the cross of Jesus Christ and uttered his faith in the striking word-picture of this hymn:

> In the cross of Christ I glory,
> Towering o'er the wrecks of time.

He lived to be over eighty years old, writing other famous hymns, among them our well-known missionary hymn, "Watchman, Tell Us of the Night." At length he died in 1872 at Exeter, his birthplace; and upon his tombstone you may read the inscription, "In the cross of Christ I glory."

56. Oft in Danger, Oft in Woe

HENRY KIRKE WHITE, 1785-1806
FRANCES SARA (FULLER-MAITLAND) COLQUHOUN, 1809-1877

Two authors are responsible for the hymn, "Oft in Danger, Oft in Woe." The first verse was written by a young man, Henry Kirke White, who died October 19, 1806, while still a student in Saint John's College, Cambridge University. The other verses were written by a fourteen-year-old girl, Frances Sara Fuller-Maitland, who successfully carried the spirit of White's fragmentary lines into the subsequent verses, first published by her mother, Mrs. Bertha Fuller-Maitland, in 1827.

White was born in Nottingham, England, March 21, 1785. Not wanting to become a butcher, like his father, he became apprenticed to a weaver when only fourteen years old, afterward entering a law office. His genius as a poet began to blossom while he was still a boy. A book of his poems that he published at the age of seventeen showed that he had become irreligious.

A dear friend of his, named Almond, had become a Christian, and told White that they could no longer associate together, because of White's scorn of the Christian life. This hurt White so deeply that he exclaimed: "You surely think worse of me than I deserve!" But Almond's courageous stand brought White to his senses, and gradually the young poet realized his lost condition and found his way to the Saviour of mankind. The story of his struggle toward the light is pictured in his hymn, "When Marshaled on the Nightly Plain." After his death in college they found on some mathematical papers his lines, beginning, "Much in sorrow, oft in woe."

57. My Country, 'Tis of Thee

SAMUEL FRANCIS SMITH, 1808-1895

A STUDENT, twenty-three years old, studying in Andover Theological Seminary for the Baptist ministry, wrote the American national hymn in less than a half hour on the second day of February, 1832. His name was Samuel F. Smith, the author also of "The Morning Light is Breaking." The words were in part inspired by the tune we call "America," which he had found in a German collection of songs loaned to him shortly before by Lowell Mason, that master editor of hymn-books in the early nineteenth century. Mason had secured the book from William C. Woodbridge.

Authorities have disagreed as to where the tune came from—whether Saxony, Russia, Sweden, or England, in all of which countries it has been popularly sung to patriotic words. Because of its striking similarity to certain ancient tunes, it has been claimed by various writers to have come from an old French tune or a still older Scottish carol. The probabilities are—and on this most editors agree today—that the first man to write the tune in nearly its present form was Henry Carey, an English composer, who lived from 1685 until 1743. Once when regret was expressed to Dr. Smith that his American national hymn is sung to the same tune as the British hymn, he replied: "I do not share this regret. On the contrary, I deem it a new and beautiful bond of union between the mother country and her daughter." The hymn was first sung July 4, 1832, at a children's patriotic celebration in Boston.

58. O Say, Can You See by the Dawn's Early Light

FRANCIS SCOTT KEY, 1779-1843

FRANCIS SCOTT KEY, author of the "Star-Spangled Banner," was born at Double Pipe Creek, Maryland, on the estate of his father, John Ross Key, an officer in the Revolutionary War. He was educated at Saint John's College, practiced law at Frederick, Maryland, and for three terms served as district attorney at Georgetown in the District of Columbia under President Andrew Jackson.

During the War of 1812 with England, Key visited the British ship, "Minden," in order to secure the release of some of the prisoners, one of them being his friend, Doctor William Beanes, of Upper Marlboro, Maryland. Merely because of his sympathy with the American cause, Doctor Beanes was held by the British. Key was successful in getting the prisoners released. But just as they were all about to depart, the British decided not to let them go that night because of the attack about to be made upon Baltimore. Accordingly, they were taken on board the frigate "Surprise" and carried up the Patapsco River to their own vessel, which was kept under guard, lest they escape and give away information to their fellow countrymen. During the battle between the ships and the forts their anxiety was intense. And as Key walked the deck, eagerly awaiting the dawn, which should tell him whether or not over Fort McHenry the flag was still there, he wrote on the back of a letter:

"O say, can you see by the dawn's early light,
  What so proudly we hailed at the twilight's last
    gleaming?"

On the rowboat that bore him shoreward in the morning he completed the song now so famous.

59. Jerusalem the Golden

BERNARD OF CLUNY, 12th Century

THE pious monk, now known as Bernard of Cluny, was born in the twelfth century in Morlaix, France; and upon maturity dedicated himself to the service of God in the Abbey of Cluny. Whether or not he was named after Saint Bernard of Clairvaux, as some suppose, it is known that he was much younger than the author of "Jesus, the Very Thought of Thee." From within the cloistered walls of the Abbey the godly man looked out upon the world about him, and was sick at heart to see so much worldliness and sin in the life of the people of his day.

As he meditated upon this sad condition, which weighed so heavily upon his soul, he wrote in the Latin language a great poem of three thousand lines, entitled, "Concerning a Disdain of the World." While it is largely a satire upon the sinful age, and warns against the wrath to come, the poem by way of contrast contains the most exalted passages, expressing the poet's eager contemplation of the glorious life awaiting the blessed in heaven. Doctor John Mason Neale, an English clergyman and scholar, has made exquisite translations into English from these lines upon heaven, and from his translations, among others, has been taken our stirring hymn, "Jerusalem, the Golden." It has been called the "Hymn of heavenly homesickness," as it expresses so tenderly the yearning of the devout soul for "that sweet and blessed country."

60. O for a Thousand Tongues to Sing

CHARLES WESLEY, 1707-1788

CHARLES WESLEY, the greatest hymn-writer in Methodist history, wrote over six thousand hymns, some of which have attained the first rank in English hymnody. He and his brother, John Wesley, admitted that they made more converts through their hymns than through their preaching.

Charles Wesley usually celebrated each anniversary of his birthday by writing a hymn of praise to God. Little wonder, therefore, that the first anniversary of his conversion, his spiritual birthday, should be celebrated by one of the most helpful hymns in use among Methodists. The opening line of the hymn, "O for a thousand tongues to sing," is reminiscent of a remark of praise to God, once uttered to Wesley by Peter Böhler: "Had I a thousand tongues, I would praise Him with them all."

When Charles Wesley was converted he had been ill in bed for some time, and the fear of death had often come to his mind. On Sunday, May 21, 1738, his brother and some friends came in and sang a hymn. After they went out he prayed alone for some time. In his journal we read: "I was composing myself to sleep in quietness and peace when I heard one come in and say, 'In the name of Jesus of Nazareth, arise, and believe, and thou shalt be healed of all thine infirmities.' The words struck me to the heart. I lay musing and trembling. With a strange palpitation of heart, I said, yet feared to say, 'I believe, I believe!'" These memories he has woven into that wonderful third verse of the hymn:

> Jesus! the name that charms our fears,
>   That bids our sorrows cease;
> 'Tis music in the sinner's ears,
>   'Tis life, and health, and peace.

61. Christians, Awake, Salute the Happy Morning

JOHN BYROM, 1692-1763

THE happy morning of Christmas, the happiest of the whole year, is associated with the giving of presents in token of the gifts borne by the three Wise Men of the East to the manger cradle. Doctor John Byrom, an English physician, who afterward became famous by inventing a system of shorthand, was an occasional contributor to the famous Spectator under the *nom de plume* "John Shadow." He was especially gifted in writing poems that reflected his kindly and happy nature.

One day in 1745 as Christmas was approaching he told his favorite daughter, Dolly Byrom, that he was making a Christmas present for her. When Christmas morning arrived he handed to her an envelope addressed to her. When she opened it, she found therein a poem for Christmas morning, written by her father, dedicated to her, and entitled "Christmas Day for Dolly." Little did either of them dream on that morning that those joyous lines would live and be sung for centuries to help gladden other Christmas mornings for generations yet unborn. The manuscript of the hymn was preserved in the Byrom family for a hundred years. It is now one of the treasures of the Chetham's Hospital, Manchester, England.

For the boys in this hospital Byrom wrote a number of hymns at various times, and once he declared that he would rather do that than be poet laureate to Frederick the Second. After his death his poems were collected and the posthumous volume, *Poems, &c.*, was published in 1773. His complete *Works* were published in 1814.

62. I'll Praise My Maker, While I've Breath

ISAAC WATTS, 1674-1748

THIS hymn, over two centuries old, was written as a metrical version of the 146th Psalm, "While I live will I praise the Lord," and was first published by Isaac Watts in 1719, under the title, "Praise to God for His Goodness and Truth" in his *Psalms of David, &c.* Seventeen years later John Wesley, then a missionary to America, was so fond of the hymn that he included it in his first hymn book, *Psalms and Hymns,* 1736-37, and in later years used it in others of his books.

This partiality for the hymn lasted throughout Wesley's life. Watts originally wrote "I'll praise my Maker with my breath," but Wesley altered this and one other line. Hymnologists disagree as to the desirability of the changes Wesley made. Doctor C. S. Robinson declared that they "were not for the better, and have only served to confuse the forms in which it appears." Doctor John Julian, editor of the monumental *Dictionary of Hymnology,* states, however, that "the more popular arrangement, which is in extensive use in all English-speaking countries, is that by J. Wesley."

Wesley gave out this hymn just before preaching for the last time in City Road Chapel, Tuesday evening, February 22, 1791. The following Monday afternoon, though very ill, he amazed the friends at his bedside by singing the hymn throughout in a strong voice. The next night, his biographer, Tyerman, tells us, he tried scores of times to repeat the hymn, but could only say "I'll praise —I'll praise——." And with praise for his Maker on his lips and in his heart he passed to that life where "immortality endures."

63. Break Thou the Bread of Life

MARY ANN LATHBURY, 1841-1913

THE great institution known as Chautauqua, founded by Lewis Miller and Doctor John H. Vincent, afterward bishop of the Methodist Episcopal Church, held its first assembly on the shores of Lake Chautauqua in the northwest part of New York State under a resolution of the Sunday School Board, adopted in October, 1873. The formal opening was held, August 4, 1874. From a small beginning it has developed into a great center for culture, religious and intellectual; and from this source streams of helpful influence have poured out into our national life through the Chautauqua Literary and Scientific Circles and the ten thousand assemblies that are annually held in this country under the name of Chautauqua.

Doctor Jesse Lyman Hurlbut, historian of Chautauqua, writes:[1]

"In Doctor Vincent's many-sided nature was a strain of poetry, although I do not know that he ever wrote a verse. Yet he always looked at life and truth through poetic eyes. Who otherwise would have thought of songs for Chautauqua and called upon a poet to write them? Doctor Vincent found in Mary A. Lathbury a poet who could compose fitting verses for the expression of the Chautauqua spirit."

In 1885 she was the founder of the Look-up Legion, based on the motto of the Henry Wadsworth Club in Edward Everett Hale's "Ten Times One Is Ten." In 1875 she wrote her first song for Chautauqua, and in 1877 penned this hymn as a study song for the Normal Classes at Chautauqua. "Beside the sea" suggests the place, and "the bread of life" the purpose, of their Bible study.

[1] From "The Story of Chautauqua" by Dr. J. L. Hurlbut. Courtesy of G. P. Putnam's Sons, Publishers, New York and London.

64. There Is a Land of Pure Delight

Isaac Watts, 1674-1748

Isaac Watts was born in Southampton on the southern coast of England. At the time of his birth his father, a staunch Nonconformist, was in prison because of his religious beliefs. So firm was he in his faith that he suffered himself to be again imprisoned for the same reason, while his son, Isaac, was still an infant. As the boy grew older he was educated in the classics by the Rector of All Saints in Southampton, and gave such promise of a brilliant future that a Southampton doctor promised to send him to the university if he would promise to become ordained as a clergyman in the Church of England. But he refused and for four years attended a Nonconformist Academy in Stoke Newington, afterward returning to Southampton for two years.

During those two years in Southampton he wrote most of the early hymns which are embodied in his famous book, *Hymns and Spiritual Songs*. From the windows of his home at Southampton there extended a beautiful view which the young man loved. Across Southampton water were seen the green fields of the Isle of Wight; and one day this fair prospect turned his thoughts toward the beauties of the heavenly land and inspired him to write, "There Is a Land of Pure Delight." The sea in the foreground suggested the lines,

> Death like a narrow sea divides
> This heavenly land from ours,

while the summer verdure of the Isle of Wight gave to him the picture,

> Sweet fields beyond the swelling flood
> Stand dressed in living green.

65. Strong Son of God, Immortal Love

ALFRED, LORD TENNYSON, 1809-1892

LIKE the friendship of David and Jonathan was the bond of intimacy between the poet Tennyson and his friend at Cambridge University, Arthur H. Hallam. A son of the famous historian, young Hallam showed unusual promise, and in his intellectual breadth, as well as in his capacity for friendly affection, he made an ideal companion for Tennyson. They became the dearest of friends, and when Arthur fell in love with the poet's younger sister, Emilia, the bonds of friendship were strengthened.

In the summer of 1830 Tennyson and Hallam made a journey together through the French Pyrenees. Three years later Hallam died in Vienna, and "to the heart of one man," as Doctor Henry van Dyke expresses it,[1] "it was the shock of an inward earthquake, upheaving the foundations of life and making the very arch of heaven tremble. . . . Tennyson felt his loss in the inmost fibers of his being. The world was changed, darkened, filled with secret conflicts. The importunate questions of human life and destiny thronged upon his soul. The ideal peace, the sweet, art-satisfied seclusion, the dreams of undisturbed repose, became impossible for him. He must fight, not for a party cause, but for spiritual freedom and immortal hopes."

Out of this sorrow came Tennyson's wonderful elegy, "In Memoriam," first published in 1850, in which he immortalized the friend of his youth, and gave to the world the highest expression of his own thought and the finest art of his poetic genius. From the third, fourth, and fifth stanzas of the prologue of "In Memoriam" this hymn was taken.

[1] From "The Poetry of Tennyson," by Henry van Dyke. Charles Scribner's Sons, Publishers.

66. Lord, I Hear of Showers of Blessing

ELIZABETH CODNER

THE author, a mission worker in London, tells this story of the origin of her hymn:

"A party of young friends over whom I was watching with anxious hope attended a meeting in which details were given of a revival work in Ireland. They came back greatly impressed. My fear was lest their own fleece remain dry, and I pressed upon them the privilege and responsibility of getting a share in the outpoured blessing. On the Sunday following, not being well enough to get out, I had a time of quiet communion. Those children were still on my heart, and I longed to press upon them an earnest individual appeal. Without effort words seemed to be given to me, and they took the form of a hymn," which as it was passed from one to another of the young people, "became a word of power."

Years later E. P. Hammond sent to her this letter which he had received:

"Thank you for singing me that hymn, 'Even Me,' for it was the singing of that hymn that saved me. I was a lost woman, a wicked mother. I have stolen and lied and been so bad to my dear, innocent children. Friendless, I attended your inquiry meeting; but no one came to me because of the crowd. But on Saturday afternoon, at the First Presbyterian Church, when they all sang that hymn together, those beautiful words, 'Let some drops now fall on me,' and also those, 'Blessing others, O bless me,' it seemed to reach my very soul. I thought, 'Jesus can accept me—"Even Me,"' and it brought me to His feet, and I feel the burden of sin removed. Can you wonder that I love those words and I love to hear them sung?"

67. O Jesus, Thou Art Standing

BISHOP WILLIAM WALSHAM HOW, 1823-1897

THE author of many theological works, Bishop How, of the Church of England, is to-day remembered by the great hymns which he gave to the Christian Church. This hymn, perhaps the most popular of them all, was inspired by reading a poem by Jean Ingelow, describing the effect upon the hearers of an earnest sermon preached by a humble minister in a fishing village. Bishop How has told in his own words how the hymn came to be written:

"I composed the hymn early in 1867, after I had been reading a very beautiful poem, entitled, 'Brothers and a Sermon.' The pathos of the verses impressed me very forcibly at the time. I read them over and over again, and finally, closing the book, I scribbled on an odd scrap of paper my first idea of the verses, beginning, 'O Jesu, Thou art standing.' I altered them a good deal subsequently, but I am fortunate in being able to say that after the hymn left my hands it was never revised or altered in any way."

Doctor C. S. Nutter, the distinguished hymnologist, is responsible for the statement that Holman Hunt's famous picture, "The Light of the World," which hangs at Keble College, Oxford, is also said to have had its influence upon the author in the writing of this hymn. The painting pictures the figure of Jesus Christ, His head crowned with thorns, standing outside a closed door upon which with one hand He is knocking for entrance, while in the other hand He bears a lighted lantern.

> O shame, thrice shame upon us,
> To keep Him standing there.

68. Jesus, Saviour, Pilot Me

EDWARD HOPPER, 1818-1888

SOMETIMES Christian hymns speak to the laboring man in the familiar terms of his daily work. Charles Wesley visited the colliers at Newcastle-on-Tyne and, seeing the reflection of their furnace-fires against the midnight sky, wrote for them the hymn, "See How Great a Flame Aspires." Likewise on visiting the quarrymen at Portland he wrote for them the hymn, containing the lines,

> Strike with the hammer of Thy Word,
> And break these hearts of stone.

It was a similar impulse that led Edward Hopper, while working among seafaring men, to write for them the hymn, "Jesus, Saviour, Pilot Me," which is full of pictures of the sea and is suggestive of the miracle wrought by Jesus Christ when He and His disciples were on the sea.

From 1870 until his death in 1888, the author, a Presbyterian clergyman, was pastor of the Church of the Sea and Land, which was largely a mission to sailors. The anniversary of the Seamen's Friend Society was held in Broadway Tabernacle, New York city, on May 10, 1880, and for that occasion he was asked to write a new hymn. Instead he brought this hymn, which he had published anonymously in the *Sailors' Magazine* in 1871, and read it to the congregation. Then for the first time the secret of its authorship became known; for it had already been printed anonymously in a number of hymnals, albeit without the knowledge of its author.

69. Come, Thou Fount of Every Blessing

ROBERT ROBINSON, 1735-1790

WHEN Robert Robinson was a very young boy his father died. At the age of fourteen Robert went to London to work for a hair-dresser. While there he fell among evil companions. One Sunday in 1752 they brought some liquor to an old woman who told fortunes, so as to enjoy a good laugh as they listened to her prophecies. When she told Robinson, however, that he would live to see his children and grandchildren, the prophecy sobered him with the thought of the responsibilities of life. Shortly afterward he heard George Whitefield preach on "The wrath to come," and fell under deep conviction which continued for three years.

At length at the age of twenty, hearing the preaching of Wesley, he came to the "Fount of every blessing" with the prayer, "Here's my heart, O take and seal it," and soon afterward he entered the ministry, beginning his work in a chapel at Mildenhall in Suffolk.

Two years later, in 1757, while pastor in Norwich, the memory of his conversion brought to his soul anew the joy of that experience, and under the influence of that memory he wrote the lines of gratefulness to God,

> Come, Thou Fount of every blessing,
> Tune my heart to sing Thy grace.

It was published the following year in Norfolk.

Years later he became careless in his conduct and while riding in a stagecoach he was reproved for his frivolity by a lady who eventually quoted this very hymn. Tears came to his eyes as he replied: "Madam, I am the poor, unhappy man who composed it; and I would give a thousand worlds, if I had them, to enjoy the feelings I had then."

77

70. Sow in the Morn Thy Seed

JAMES MONTGOMERY, 1771-1854

ONE day in the month of February, 1832, James Montgomery, on the way to the city of Bath, was journeying from Gloucester to Tewkesbury with his friend, Rowland Hodgson. As they rode along they passed a field where a number of women and girls were working in rows. Stopping to inquire what they were doing, the travelers were told that after digging little holes in the ground they dropped a few seeds into each hole. This process, known as "dibbling," had never been seen by Montgomery before, and he remarked: "Give me broadcast sowing, scattering the seed on the right hand and on the left in liberal handfuls!"

How this led to the writing of this hymn Montgomery has told us in his own words:

"I fell immediately into a musing fit, and moralized most magnificently upon all kinds of husbandry (though I knew little or nothing of any, but so much the better, perhaps, for my purpose), making out that each was excellent in its way, and best in its place. By degrees my thoughts subsided into verse, and I found them running lines, like furrows, along the field of my imagination: and in the course of the next two stages they had already assumed the form of the following stanzas, which I wrote as soon as we reached Bromsgrove."

The hymn was used that same year at Whitsuntide at the festival of the Sheffield Sunday School Union, for which Montgomery wrote a hymn every year for nearly forty years.

71. Glorious Things of Thee Are Spoken

JOHN NEWTON, 1725-1807

WHEN John Newton, an English preacher of the eighteenth century, in his old age could no longer read his texts, he was urged to give up preaching. "What!" said he, "shall the old African blasphemer stop while he can speak?" And in these words he correctly characterized himself as he had been before conversion. Newton could never forget that the grace of God had rescued him from the depths of sin. His godly mother had taught him the Scriptures. But she died when he was only seven years old, and at the age of eleven he went to sea with his father. His life as a sailor was full of exciting adventures and full of wickedness. He became a sea captain and a slave-trader, and was enslaved himself for a time. For years the only good influence that he knew came through his love for his future wife, Mary Catlett.

One frightful night, when he was twenty-three years old, the waterlogged vessel he was steering was almost lost. Thus facing death all night long, he surrendered his life to Jesus Christ and turned away from his sins. Later he came under the influence of Whitefield and the Wesleys, entered the Christian ministry, and lived a life of wide usefulness in the service of the Master. His influence lives to-day chiefly in the hymns that he wrote, many of them being first published with those of Cowper in the *Olney Hymns* and similar collections. His hymn, "Glorious Things of Thee Are Spoken," which we sing to the Austrian national tune, is one of the finest hymns of praise in the English language.

79

72. Hark, My Soul! It Is the Lord

WILLIAM COWPER, 1731-1800

WILLIAM COWPER is regarded as the greatest English poet who has contributed any considerable number of hymns to the wealth of our English hymnody. His life was one of great suffering and was tragic to a high degree. His early school life was extremely unhappy. Later, while studying law, he fell in love with Theodora Cowper, who was his own cousin. His devotion to her he expressed in several love poems. But to Cowper's great sorrow their marriage was forbidden by her father. The disease of melancholia fastened itself upon his mind, and his sufferings became most acute.

Though he recovered, his life was beclouded throughout by his mental depression, and he occasionally lapsed into the most desperate forms of melancholy.

Despite his great affliction, he wrote many of our most beloved hymns. His association with John Newton stimulated his interest in hymn-writing, even though it may not have added much wholesome cheer to his darkened soul. The hymn, "Hark, My Soul! It is the Lord," is perhaps the tenderest that fell from his pen. The last verse expresses simply, but exquisitely, the anxieties and yearnings of his spiritual life:

> Lord, it is my chief complaint
> That my love is weak and faint;
> Yet I love Thee and adore:
> Oh for grace to love Thee more!

73. Sun of My Soul, Thou Saviour Dear

JOHN KEBLE, 1792-1866

ONE of the literary landmarks of the early nineteenth century, in sacred poetry, at least, was *The Christian Year,* the work of the Rev. John Keble. A high churchman of the Church of England, he was one of the founders of the Tractarian Movement, which aimed at producing a higher spiritual condition within the church. At one time he was professor of poetry in Oxford University.

From his *Christian Year* was taken our hymn, "Sun of My Soul, Thou Saviour Dear," which was part of a long hymn entitled "Evening."

In *Famous Hymns of the World,* Allan Sutherland tells this story of Keble's hymn: "In a wild night a gallant ship went to her doom. A few women and children were placed in a boat, without oars or sails, and drifted away at the mercy of the waves. Earlier in the evening, before the darkness had quite settled down, brave men on the shore had seen the peril of the vessel and had put out in the face of the tempest, hoping to save human life, but even the ship could not be found. After fruitless search, they were about returning to the shore, when out on the water, and above the wail of the storm, they heard a woman's clear voice singing:

> 'Sun of my soul, Thou Saviour dear,
> It is not night, if Thou be near.'

The work of rescue was quickly accomplished. But for the singing, in all probability, this boatload of lives would have drifted beyond human help or been dashed to pieces before morning."

74. The Morning Light Is Breaking

SAMUEL FRANCIS SMITH, 1808-1895

THIS missionary hymn of optimism and of challenge to the Christian Church was written in the same year and by the same author as our national hymn, "My Country, 'Tis of Thee." The author was the Rev. Samuel Francis Smith, of whom his classmate in Harvard University, Dr. Oliver Wendell Holmes, wrote in the Class Poem of 1829:

> And there's a fine youngster of excellent pith,
> Fate tried to conceal him by naming him Smith.

The year of its composition was 1832, when the author graduated from Andover Theological Seminary, entered the Baptist ministry, and became editor of the Baptist Missionary Magazine. Little wonder that he should have written a missionary hymn in a year of such missionary interest to himself!

The hymn was first published in a hymnal that was under preparation that same year, Hastings' *Spiritual Songs.* In 1843 the author included it in a collection of hymns, entitled *The Psalmist,* which he and Baron Stow prepared for American Baptists—a hymnal that achieved wide popularity.

Though Doctor Smith two years later left the missionary editorship to enter the pastorate at Waterville, Maine, he did not lose his intense interest in missions. And so after his pastorate in Newton, Massachusetts, we find him editor of the publications of the Baptist Missionary Union. Having traveled widely among the foreign missions, Doctor Smith was enabled to write that his hymn "has been a great favorite at missionary gatherings, and I myself heard it sung in five or six different languages in Europe and Asia."

75. Take My Life, and Let It Be

FRANCES RIDLEY HAVERGAL, 1836-1879

OF this hymn, written while visiting Areley House, in England, 1874, the author, Frances Ridley Havergal, once wrote: "There were ten persons in the house, some unconverted and long prayed for; some converted, but not rejoicing Christians. He gave me the prayer: 'Lord, give me all in this house.' And He just DID! Before I left the house everyone had got a blessing. The last night of my visit, after I had retired, the governess asked me to go to the two daughters. They were crying, etc. Then and there both of them trusted and rejoiced. It was nearly midnight. I was too happy to sleep, and passed most of the night in praise and renewal of my own consecration; and these little couplets formed themselves and chimed in my heart one after another until they finished with 'Ever, only, all for Thee!'"

Four years later she wrote: "The Lord has shown me another little step, and of course I have taken it with extreme delight. 'Take my silver and my gold' now means shipping off all my ornaments (including a jewel cabinet, which is really fit for a countess) to the Church Missionary House, where they will be accepted and disposed of for me. I retain only a brooch or two for daily wear, which are memorials of my dear parents; also a locket with the only portrait I have of my niece, who is in heaven. But these I redeem so that the whole value goes to the Church Missionary Society."

76. I Think, When I Read That Sweet Story of Old

JEMIMA LUKE, 1813-1906

JEMIMA THOMPSON, who afterward married the Rev. Samuel Luke, wrote this hymn in 1841. Like many hymns, it was partly inspired by a tune— in this case a Greek melody—the pathos of which stirred the author's fancy as she read it at the Normal Infant School at Gray's Inn Road. She once wrote: "I went one day on some missionary business to the little town of Wellington, five miles from Faunton, in a stagecoach. It was a beautiful spring morning; it was an hour's ride and there was no other inside passenger. On the back of an old envelope I wrote in pencil the first two of the verses now so well known. . . . The third verse was added afterward to make it a missionary hymn."

One day a newsboy in New York entered a bank with a bundle of papers under his arm and asked two gentlemen sitting before a fire: "Papers, sirs? Three more banks down!" "No," replied one of them, "we don't want any. But, stop! If you will sing us a song we will buy one." The boy agreed; and, expecting to hear a jovial song, they placed the little ten-year old on a table. But he surprised them by singing, "I Think, When I Read That Sweet Story of Old." Soon they were both in tears. They bought his papers and took his name and address; and the song of the Sunday school lad turned their thoughts to the olden story, "When Jesus was here among men."

77.   A Mighty Fortress Is Our God

MARTIN LUTHER, 1483-1546

THIS great war song of the Reformation, written by Martin Luther, has heartened many a German army going into battle, and has given courage to many a son of Germany amid the hardships of strange lands. It was sung every day by Luther and his friends. Before the battle of Leipzig, September 17, 1631, the whole army of Gustavus Adolphus sang the hymn.

The story is still repeated by the Germans of Herkimer County, New York, of John Christian Bush, who settled there with his family of six children and founded the village of Shell's Bush. On the afternoon of August 6, 1781, a band of Indians, led by Donald McDonald, a Scotch refugee, attacked the village. Bush, who was working in the field when they came, hurriedly assembled his people within his block-house, all except two of his children who were captured by the Indians. All afternoon and far into the night they fought furiously, Bush's wife doing valiant service in loading the guns, so that the men might never be empty-handed. Each time the Indians attacked the door they were forced back. Once they broke down the door, but the quick firing halted them. McDonald was wounded and dragged within the fort by the Germans, and the Indians fled. Then the patriots sang:

"A mighty fortress is our God,
A bulwark never failing."

Again the Indians attacked and again were repulsed, while Bush and his victorious neighbors sang the rest of the hymn as a pæan of thankfulness to God for preserving their lives in the midst of peril.

85

78. Praise God, From Whom All Blessings Flow

BISHOP THOMAS KEN, 1637-1710

THE doxology of praise to the Holy Trinity was written by the Rev. Thomas Ken, whom King Charles II once made a chaplain to his sister, Mary, Princess of Orange. Ken was so courageous in his preaching at court that the king often said on the way to chapel: "I must go and hear Ken tell me my faults."

Bishop McCabe said that while the prisoners of the Union Army during the Civil War were incarcerated in Libby Prison, day after day they saw comrades passing away and their numbers increased by living recruits. One night, about ten o'clock, through the darkness they heard the tramp of feet that soon stopped before the prison door, until arrangements could be made inside. In the company was a young Baptist minister, whose heart almost fainted when he looked on those cold walls and thought of the suffering inside. Tired and weary, he sat down, put his face in his hands, and wept. Just then a lone voice sang out from an upper window, "Praise God, from whom all blessings flow"; a dozen joined in the second line, more than a score in the third line, and the words, "Praise Father, Son, and Holy Ghost," were sung by nearly all the prisoners. As the song died away on the still night, the young man arose and sang:

"Prisons would palaces prove,
    If Jesus would dwell with me there."

79. What a Friend We Have in Jesus

Joseph Scriven, 1820-1886

ONE of the most helpful hymns in popular use is Joseph Scriven's hymn on the friendship of Jesus, the comforter and burden-bearer. Scriven was a native of Dublin, Ireland, born in 1820. He graduated from Trinity College in his native city. At the age of twenty-five he emigrated to Canada, and lived there until his death at Port Hope on Lake Ontario, October 10, 1886.

When a young man, he was engaged to be married to a lady whom he had known and loved for a long time. All preparations had been made for the wedding ceremony and the date had been fixed. But shortly before the wedding day arrived his promised bride was accidentally drowned, and he was plunged into the deepest sorrow. From this sad experience came a deep sense of his dependence upon Christ and of the great truth so helpfully expressed in his lines:

> What a Friend we have in Jesus,
> All our sins and griefs to bear!

Out of the intense sympathy wrought in his heart by this experience, he wrote the hymn to comfort his mother in her own sorrow and sent it to her in Ireland. How it came to be first published is not known, as he had not intended it for general use. Indeed, for some time after it was printed its authorship was unknown, being sometimes incorrectly attributed to Doctor Horatius Bonar. After Scriven's death, however, he became recognized as the author of the hymn that has blessed so many thousands of believers.

80.   O God, My Powers Are Thine

FREDERICK WATSON HANNAN, 1865-

THE Rev. Frederick Watson Hannan, now professor of pastoral theology in Drew Theological Seminary, Madison, New Jersey, was for eight years the pastor of the Bushwick Avenue Central Methodist Episcopal Church, Brooklyn, New York city, which has a Sunday school of over thirty-three hundred enrolled members. Each fall during Doctor Hannan's pastorate there it was the custom to observe Sunday School Day as a Rally Day when special exercises were held not only in the school, but also in the morning congregational service. A sermon was preached especially to the teachers, and a service of responsive readings was prepared, in which the pastor and teachers took part. After the sermon a consecration service for the teachers was held, and for this service Doctor Hannan always wrote a hymn, which was sung by the teachers as they stood around the altar. The whole service was very impressive.

The hymn, "O God, My Powers Are Thine," was the consecration hymn used on September 24, 1905, and was especially written for that occasion. In the current hymnals it is printed almost exactly as it was in the weekly church calendar of that date. Now this hymn is being used every year in similar consecration services for Sunday school teachers, for it breathes in song the highest ideals of self-surrender to God, which is the first condition for effective service in the work of all truly devoted Sunday school teachers.

81. Alas! and Did My Saviour Bleed?

ISAAC WATTS, 1674-1748

ENTITLED, "Godly Sorrow Arising From the Sufferings of Christ," and first published in the first edition of *Hymns and Spiritual Songs* in 1707, this hymn has in the intervening two centuries been the means of leading many a wandering sinner in repentance to the foot of the cross. The great evangelist, E. P. Hammond, when a boy of seventeen years, in Southington, Connecticut, was converted through the singing of these lines, although it was not during any special evangelistic meetings, such as he himself conducted so successfully in the years that followed.

The blind hymn-writer, Fanny Crosby, tells of her conversion in the old Thirtieth Street Methodist Episcopal Church, New York city, in November, 1850: "After a prayer was offered, they began to sing the grand old consecration hymn, 'Alas! and Did My Saviour Bleed?' and when they reached the third line of the fifth stanza, 'Here, Lord, I give myself away,' my very soul flooded with celestial light."

Doctor C. S. Robinson in his *Annotations Upon Popular Hymns* has made this comment on the hymn:

"In the third stanza there has always been one line which the Christians on both sides of the ocean, and of every denomination, have been reluctant to receive. Doctor Watts wrote it thus: 'When God, the Mighty Maker, dy'd.' Now, when we remember that this revered author has been violently accused of being so Unitarian in sentiment that Scottish Presbyterians cannot sing his versions of Psalms, even at Pan-Presbyterian councils, it is refreshing to hear him assert such doctrinal extravagance in his zeal to be orthodox."

82. The Sands of Time Are Sinking

ANNE ROSS COUSIN, 1824-1906

BECAUSE of his deep piety and the triumphant spirit with which he bore his many persecutions, Samuel Rutherford (1600-1661) is remembered as one of the Christian martyrs of Scotland. Dean Stanley called him "the true saint of the Covenant." Based upon his words, and especially those uttered upon his death-bed, this hymn was written by the wife of a Presbyterian minister after an appreciative study of Rutherford's life.

Rutherford was a learned professor of theology and a minister of the gospel, beginning his pastoral work at Anworth in 1627. Ten years later he wrote to John Gordon: "My worthy and dear brother, misspend not your short sandglass which runneth very fast; seek your Lord in time." These words form the theme of the opening lines of the hymn.

He was so steadfast in beliefs that conflicted with the orthodoxy of his time that in 1636 he was brought before the High Commission Court, removed from his church and banished to Aberdeen. Later his books were burned under his windows at Saint Andrews, and finally after the Restoration he was summoned for high treason before Parliament. But the approach of death intervened and he wrote in reply: "I am summoned before a higher Judge and judicatory, . . . and ere a few days arrive I shall be where few kings and great folks come."

In reply to the question, "What think ye now of Christ?" his dying words were: "I shall live and adore Him. Glory, glory to my Creator and Redeemer forever. Glory shineth on Immanuel's land." These and others of his utterances Mrs. Cousin wove into a poem of nineteen stanzas, from which this hymn and also that beginning, "Oh, Christ, He is the fountain," were taken.

83. Art Thou Weary, Art Thou Languid?

SAINT STEPHEN, THE SABAITE, 725-794
(Translated by John Mason Neale, 1818-1866)

A GREEK hymn of the eighth century, the original lines of this poem by Saint Stephen the Sabaite so appealed to the great translator, Doctor Neale, that he wrote of them that they "strike me as being very sweet." He made so free a translation from the Greek, however, that the English version almost deserves to be classed as an original hymn.

Stephen's uncle, Saint John of Damascus, placed him in the monastery at Mar Saba in the wilderness of Judæa near the Dead Sea, when the latter was only ten years old. Eventually he became a monk of Sabas and remained there for fifty-nine years until his death. At an early age he came under the influence of Cosmas, who guided and perfected his literary style, so that he became a poet and thus learned to give noble expression to his devout meditations. The most beautiful of his poems is this hymn, which has endured for nearly eleven centuries.

The monastery also still stands, "clinging to the face of a steep precipice, so that it is difficult to distinguish man's masonry from the natural rock." It is visited by travelers in the Holy Land, and the Rev. James King in his *Anglican Hymnology* (1885) gives an interesting account of it. The forty monks now there hold seven religious services daily. After being shown "their gayly decorated chapel, the tomb of Saint Sabas, the tomb of Saint John of Damascus, and a cave containing thousands of skulls of martyred monks," Doctor King was led to the belfry on the roof, where he "saw the bells which send forth their beautiful chimes and gladden the hearts of pilgrims who, 'weary and languid,' pursue their journey through the desolate wilderness."

84. The Day of Wrath, That Dreadful Day

THOMAS OF CELANO, ?-1255
(Translated by Sir Walter Scott, 1771-1832)

THE stately solemnity of the ancient poem on the
Judgment Day, the greatest of all the Latin hymns,
first resounded through the soul of an obscure
monk, Thomas, born in the Italian town of Celano.
He was a friend of Saint Francis of Assisi. It has
been said of Dante, "He has seen hell." Likewise,
of Thomas it has been said by Macdonald, the
English hymnologist, "He has seen the great, white
throne and Him that sits upon it." The lofty theme
and the literary perfection with which the thrilling
lines have given it utterance have been the admira-
tion of the Christian Church throughout many ages.

Numberless translations have been made, but few
have approached in beauty the condensed translation
which Sir Walter Scott made and introduced into
The Lay of the Last Minstrel at the climax wherein
he describes a pilgrimage to Melrose Abbey for the
purpose of praying for the repose of the soul of
Michael Scott.

> And ever in the office close
> The hymn of intercession rose;
> And far the echoing aisles prolong
> The awful burthen of the song—
> *Dies irae, dies illa.*

Mr. Gladstone once said of it: "I know of nothing more sublime in the writings of Sir Walter
Scott—certainly I know nothing so sublime in any
portion of the sacred poetry of modern times."

Sir Walter's biographer, Lockhart, in describing
the scenes at the death-bed of the Scottish bard, tells
of how frequently he quoted fragments of the Bible,
or some petition in the Litany, or a Scotch metrical
version of a psalm or "some of the magnificent
hymns of the Romish ritual"; and he adds, "We
often heard distinctly the cadence of the *Dies Irae.*"

85. O King of Kings, O Lord of Hosts

HENRY BURTON, 1840-

IN *The Christian Advocate* Doctor Burton's daughter gives this account of her father's famous hymn:

"In 1887 Doctor Burton was one of three to be asked to write an ode for the jubilee of Queen Victoria. It was set to music by Sir John Stainer, and sung at a special festival of the National Children's Home and Orphanage, in the Royal Albert Hall, London, by a choir of a thousand voices, accompanied by an orchestra of seventy instruments, Madame Antoinette Stirling and Mr. John Pobert taking the solos. Sir John Stainer afterward wrote Doctor Burton, asking if he could not put it in another form which would be suitable for any occasion, and he would adapt the music to it. This Doctor Burton did, and the hymn was evolved which has been described as the finest national anthem of modern times."

Doctor John Telford, in his *The Methodist Hymn-Book Illustrated,* tells us that Stainer in his letter to Doctor Burton stated that he was much delighted with the words and regretted that they would cease to be "current coin" when the Jubilee was over; adding: "If you like the music I wrote, would it be possible to write a few verses of a patriotic hymn to the tune? I admire the bold rhythm of your first verse and venture to suggest that if that portion of the music were wedded to another set of words, both might live a little longer than this year."

The tune, composed by Stainer for this hymn, was "Rex Regum."

Doctor Burton, a Wesleyan Methodist clergyman in West Kirby, England, was educated in America (Beloit College). This and his other hymns have given him a foremost place among modern hymnists.

93

86. Faith of Our Fathers: Living Still

FREDERICK WILLIAM FABER, 1814-1863

THE singing of hymns to the "Lord and Master of us all" is the greatest bond between Christians of different forms of faith. Evangelical churches sing hymns by the Unitarian poets, such as Sir John Bowring's "In the Cross of Christ I Glory," and Sarah Flower Adams's "Nearer, My God, to Thee," and the Roman Catholic hymns of Father Faber, and Cardinal Newman's "Lead, Kindly Light"; while Charles Wesley's "Jesus, Lover of My Soul," and "Onward, Christian Soldiers," by Sabine Baring-Gould, are sung with fervor by Romanists.

It is curious that just as Faber, once a priest in the Church of England, in sympathy with the Oxford Movement, followed Newman in 1846 into the Roman Catholic Church, his hymn, "Faith of Our Fathers," has traveled in the opposite direction, and by an editorial modification of its theological teaching has been changed from an expression of Romanist faith into one of the great war-songs of modern Protestantism. Faber wrote, having distinctly in mind the heroes and martyrs of Catholicism:

> Faith of our fathers! living still
>   In spite of dungeon, fire, and sword,
> How Ireland's heart beats high with joy.

His lines, uttering the Mariolatry of his Church,

> Faith of our fathers! Mary's prayers
>   Shall win our country back to thee,

were altered in a Unitarian hymnal to

> Faith of our fathers! Good men's prayers
>   Shall win our country all to thee.

He states in his Preface to *Jesus and Mary*, in which this hymn first appeared, that his purpose was to supply Catholic hymns with the fervor and simplicity of the *Olney Hymns* and the Wesley hymns.

94

87. Through the Night of Doubt and Sorrow

BERNHARDT SEVERIN INGEMANN, 1789-1862
(Translated by Sabine Baring-Gould, 1834-)

RECEIVING their inspiration first from the famous Petersen brothers, Olaf and Lars, who heartened the reform movement in Sweden by their spiritual songs in the early sixteenth century, Scandinavian hymns have been distinctly subjective in character, and have expressed the sentiments and religious experience of the individual worshipers far more than the elements of faith and its objective expressions.

An excellent example of this has been the hymn, "Through the Night of Doubt and Sorrow," first written in the Danish language by Professor Ingemann. A famous poet, and thereby greatly endeared to his own people, he began his career as a lawyer, and later abandoned law for literature. He was for forty years, 1822-1862, Professor of the Danish Language and Literature in the Academy of Sorö, Zealand, Denmark. In 1851 his collected works were published in thirty-four volumes, including a series of historical romances dealing with Danish life in the Middle Ages.

His great popularity, however, was based chiefly on his hymns and songs, written especially for children. Once, upon his birthday, the children of Denmark, holding him in great affection, gathered a large fund by small subscriptions and presented him with a golden horn.

In 1825 he published his *High-Mass Hymns*. In 1842 in the Supplement to this book he included a hymn, written for the Second Sunday in Advent, based on Romans 5. 4, and picturing the journey of Israel through the wilderness. Doctor Sabine Baring-Gould translated it into English, and thus was born our hymn, "Through the Night of Doubt and Sorrow."

88. The Spacious Firmament on High

JOSEPH ADDISON, 1672-1719

THE Hebrew Psalms formed the oldest hymn book of worship to the living God. Sung antiphonally by worshipers through thousands of years, they have carried the singers through noble thought and exalted emotion into the very presence of Deity. Could hymnology give to us the story of David's experiences inspiring the composition of those Psalms which fell from his pen, we might discover that it was in his early days at Bethlehem as a shepherd boy, watching over his flocks by night, that he learned to love the stars bestudding the clear oriental sky, and to understand their message of the infinite wisdom and greatness of God.

Psalm 19, beginning with the majestic lines, "The heavens declare the glory of God; and the firmament sheweth his handywork," was Joseph Addison's inspiration in writing his great hymn, "The Spacious Firmament on High." Like his "Traveler's Hymn," "How are Thy servants blest, O Lord" (*q. v.*), and "When All Thy Mercies, O My God," this hymn was first published as a climax to one of his essays in The Spectator.

It appeared on Saturday, August 23, 1712, in No. 465, at the end of an essay on faith. After a quotation from Psalm 19, the author introduces the hymn with these words: "As such a bold and sublime manner of Thinking furnished out very noble Matter for an Ode, the Reader may see it wrought into the following one."

Dr. Samuel Johnson was very fond of quoting the hymn. Hartley Coleridge, however, objecting to "the spangles" and "the shining frame," once said: "They remind me of tambour work. Perhaps if I had never read the Psalm, I might think the verses fine." But nevertheless the hymn still holds an important place in Christian worship.

96

89. Rock of Ages, Cleft for Me

AUGUSTUS MONTAGUE TOPLADY, 1740-1778

THE author, the Rev. Augustus M. Toplady, bitterly opposed the doctrines preached by the Wesleys, who lived at the same time, but his sincere Christian piety produced this great hymn, that has become endeared to many generations of Wesleyan followers.

Years ago the steamer Sewanhaka burned at sea. One of the Fisk Jubilee singers was aboard. Before jumping into the sea he fastened life preservers on himself and his wife; but some one snatched hers away from her. In the water, however, she put her hands on his shoulders and thus kept afloat until, almost exhausted, she said to her husband, "I cannot hold on any longer!" "Try a little longer," begged the agonized husband. "Let us sing 'Rock of Ages.'" And as the hymn rang out over the waves, others almost sinking took up the strains of the pleading prayer to God. The hymn seemed to give new strength to many in that desperate hour. By and by a boat was seen approaching, and as it came nearer the singing was renewed until with superhuman efforts they laid hold upon the lifeboats and were carried to safety. The singer, in telling this story himself, declared that he believed this hymn had saved many lives, besides his own and his wife's, in that dreadful disaster.

Likewise, hundreds of stories might be told of the saving of souls spiritually through the helpful ministries of this, one of the greatest hymns ever penned in the English language.

90. Abide with Me: Fast Falls the Eventide
HENRY FRANCIS LYTE, 1793-1847

THE spirit of the walk of Christ with the disciples to Emmaus at eventide is reproduced in the hymn, "Abide with Me." This has been sung at the close of many a day, and, indeed, of many a Christian life, as believers have uttered it as a prayer for the presence of Christ. It was composed one Sabbath evening in 1847 out of a deep sadness that had settled down upon its author, the Rev. Henry F. Lyte. He had conducted his last communion service that day at the close of a pastorate of twenty-four years at Brixham, England. A fatal illness had already seized him and he was about to leave England to prolong his life, if possible, in the South. Toward evening he walked down his garden path to the seaside, and there thought out the imagery and many of the lines of his famous hymn. Into this he has woven the sense of change and of helplessness that one must feel in the presence of death, and also the trustful dependence upon Jesus Christ, the "Help of the helpless," which every true Christian must feel in that solemn hour. Returning to his home, he wrote out the hymn, perfecting its lines and giving to the Christian world one of its tenderest prayer-hymns. He left at once for the south of France, and soon after his arrival in Nice his strength failed him, and whispering the words, "Peace! Joy!" while he was pointing his hand upward, he died.

Heaven's morning breaks, and earth's vain shadows flee;
In life, in death, O Lord, abide with me!

Nurse Cavell, martyred in Belgium during the World War, October 15, 1915, joined the British chaplain softly in this hymn shortly before she was shot.

91.   Christ for the World We Sing

SAMUEL WOLCOTT, 1813-1886

THE influence of a motto or slogan when used as a rallying cry in a campaign can scarcely be measured. Many a political election has been determined by the popularity of some striking phrase. In many a war an army has been inspirited by a battle cry, such as, "On to Richmond!" Church workers have recognized the inspiration of the "Look up! Lift up!" motto in Epworth League work, and of "The Evangelization of the World in this Generation" in missionary work.

This hymn was suggested and partly inspired by just such a motto, which had been adopted by the Young Men's Christian Association of Ohio. And at their meeting on February 7, 1869, this motto was woven into a legend of evergreen letters over the pulpit of the church where they met: "CHRIST FOR THE WORLD AND THE WORLD FOR CHRIST."

There was a clergyman in attendance upon that meeting, a native of South Windsor, Connecticut, by the name of Dr. Samuel Wolcott. He had been a missionary to Syria and also pastor of several Congregational churches in New England and elsewhere. He was nearly fifty-six years old, and though he had not done much hymn-writing up to that time, before he died seventeen years later he had written over two hundred hymns. So impressed was he on this occasion by the motto, and by all that was said and done during the meeting to reenforce it, that on his way home from the service, walking through the streets, he composed the hymn, "Christ for the World We Sing."

92. Forward! Be Our Watchword

HENRY ALFORD, 1810-1871

DEAN HENRY ALFORD stood forth as one of the great ecclesiastical scholars of his generation. Twenty years of scholarly labor he devoted to his edition of the Greek New Testament, and accomplished besides a great wealth of literary labors, including many original hymns and translations of hymns. Probably his most popular hymn is, "Forward! be our watchword." The great Dean of Canterbury, shortly before his death, was requested by the Rev. J. G. Wood to write a hymn to be sung at the tenth festival of parochial choirs of the Canterbury Diocesan Union on June 6, 1871. His first hymn so written did not seem to Mr. Wood to be adaptable to processional use; and he suggested that the Dean go into the cathedral and march up and down the aisles, and so compose the processional hymn. Accordingly, the old Dean went into the stately cathedral, and, slowly marching beneath the high-vaulted roof and past the ancient shrines of Canterbury, where many of England's greatest men are sepulchered, he composed, while joining his voice to his steps, the hymn,

> Forward! be our watchword,
> Steps and voices joined.

It was sung by the Canterbury choirs at their festival, but before that day had come the Dean had passed on to the higher life, pressing

> Forward through the darkness
> Forward into light!

93. Come, Thou Almighty King

AUTHOR UNKNOWN

THE national hymn of England, "God Save Our Gracious King," is supposed to have been published first in 1743 or 1744. Within a couple of years, sung to the melody to which we Americans sing "My Country, 'Tis of Thee," it attained great popularity and gradually, by virtue of its widespread use, became known as the English national hymn.

Whenever a song gains universal favor many parodies and imitations are based upon it; and our hymn, "Come, Thou Almighty King," was written shortly afterward in imitation of "God Save the King" in both meter and style. Though it is attributed to Charles Wesley in many hymnals, the author is really unknown.

In the days of the American Revolution a congregation of patriotic colonists were worshiping in their church on Long Island when the service was interrupted by the arrival of a company of Hessian troops. The captain stalked up the aisle and commanded the people to sing "God Save the King." The organist started the tune that we call "America"; but the people, true to the cause of the American colonies and to their God, sang this hymn:

"Come, Thou *Almighty* King,
Help us *Thy* name to sing."

And the soldiers withdrew without enforcing their demands.

94. He Leadeth Me: O Blessed Thought:

JOSEPH HENRY GILMORE, 1834-

DR. JOSEPH H. GILMORE, the son of a governor of New Hampshire, began his career as pastor of a Baptist church, later becoming professor of Hebrew in Rochester Theological Seminary and afterward professor of English literature in Rochester University, New York. In 1862, the year of his ordination, he was visiting in Philadelphia and conducted the Wednesday evening prayer meeting in the First Baptist Church of that city. He took for his subject the Twenty-third Psalm, that most beloved hymn from the world's first hymn book. After the meeting Doctor Gilmore wrote this hymn on the text, "He leadeth me beside the still waters." It came as a result of a conversation in the home he was visiting that evening on the theme of the prayer meeting. Doctor Gilmore has described the occasion thus: "During the conversation, the blessedness of God's leadership so grew upon me that I took out my pencil, wrote the hymn just as it stands to-day, handed it to my wife, and thought no more about it. She sent it, without my knowledge, to the *Watchman and Recorder*. Three years later I went to Rochester to preach for the Second Baptist Church. On entering the chapel, I took up a hymn book, thinking, 'I wonder what they sing?' The book opened at 'He Leadeth Me!' and that was the first time I knew my hymn had found a place among the songs of the church."

95. Hail to the Lord's Anointed

JAMES MONTGOMERY, 1771-1854

JAMES MONTGOMERY, born in Scotland, the son of a Moravian clergyman, was an editor by profession. Though as a child he had joined the Moravian Church, he lost his early piety when he became a young man; but later in life he was converted and joined the Moravian Church again at the age of forty-three. Thus he became a Christian warrior, such as he describes, standing

> In all the armor of his God;
> The Spirit's sword is in his hand,
> His feet are with the gospel shod.

He and Cowper hold the foremost place among laymen of the church who are eminent hymnwriters.

His hymn, "Hail to the Lord's Anointed," he wrote in 1821, seven years after he joined the church a second time. It is a metrical version of the Seventy-second Psalm. It was written as a Christmas hymn and was first sung on Christmas Day, 1821, at a great convocation of Moravians in their settlement at Fulneck. At a Wesleyan missionary meeting, held in Liverpool on April 14 of the following year, 1822, when Doctor Adam Clarke presided, Montgomery made an address and closed it by the recital of this hymn with all of its verses, some of which are omitted in this hymnal. Doctor Clarke later used it in his famous Commentary in connection with his discussion of the Seventy-second Psalm.

96. We Plow the Fields, and Scatter

MATTHIAS CLAUDIUS, 1740-1815
(Translated by Jane Montgomery Campbell, 1817-1878)

FROM the German have been translated many of our richest hymns. Most of John Wesley's hymns in use now are those which he has translated from German hymns, and chiefly those expressing the mystical faith of the Moravians. This harvest hymn of thanksgiving, "We plow the fields, and scatter," was translated from the German hymn of Matthias Claudius by Miss Jane Montgomery Campbell in 1861. She was the daughter of an English clergyman, and he was the son of a German clergyman. Claudius lived to be seventy-four years old and died in 1815, two years before Miss Campbell was born.

This hymn was freely translated from a portion of a longer poem of seventeen verses with chorus. It appeared first in a sketch called Paul Erdmann's Feast. It was represented as the song that was sung at Paul's home by the peasants after the harvest was over.

As may be inferred from this hymn, there was a wholesome cheer in the author's writings as well as in his life, and this in spite of the fact that he was not unaccustomed to hardships. Menzel has said of him that his genius never reached its fullest development because he was constantly harassed by his poverty. But he was a man of great piety, and his influence for good was very considerable. He chose to dwell upon the blessings with which God enriches us, and from his very heart he sang:

> We thank Thee, then, O Father,
> For all things bright and good.

97. The God of Abraham Praise

THOMAS OLIVERS, 1725-1799

THOMAS OLIVERS, when a boy orphaned and friendless, fell into the company of bad companions and won the reputation of being "the worst boy in that country in thirty years." As a man, he learned the trade of a shoemaker, but continued in his wicked ways, until at last the preaching of Whitefield got hold upon his soul, stirring him with a message from the text, "Is not this a brand plucked out of the fire?"

Olivers became converted, and immediately set about helping the Wesleys in the work of plucking other brands from the fire. He assisted in setting up type for the Wesleyan publications, he became an efficient preacher and, as is evidenced by this wonderful hymn, a hymn-writer of a high order.

One night in London, he was attracted to a service in a Jewish synagogue, where he heard a great singer, Leoni, sing an ancient Hebrew melody in the solemn, plaintive mode and he became impressed with a desire to write a hymn to that tune. The result was our hymn, "The God of Abraham Praise," which is in a sense a paraphrase of the ancient Hebrew Yigdal, or doxology, though Olivers gave to it a distinctly Christian flavor.

The story is told of a young Jewess who had been baptized into the Christian faith, and in consequence was abandoned by her family. She fled to the home of the minister, poured out her heart to him, and as if to show that, after all, her joy in her new-found Saviour was greater than all her loss of home and family, she sang, "The God of Abraham Praise."

98. Nearer, My God, to Thee

SARAH FLOWER ADAMS, 1805-1848

BENJAMIN FLOWER in 1798 published an article in the Cambridge Intelligencer, attacking the attitude of Bishop Watson toward the French Revolution, and so offended the reverend gentleman that Flower was cast into prison. Among those who visited him in prison to sympathize with him was Miss Eliza Gould, who met him there for the first time. After his release they were married. Their youngest child, Sarah, became Mrs. Sarah Flower Adams; and by that name she is known as the author of "Nearer, My God, to Thee."

In 1841, deeply impressed by the story in Genesis of Jacob's vision at Bethel of the ladder to heaven with angels ascending and descending thereon, she wrote her hymn that has since become so universally popular and helpful.

The Rev. Doctor Millard F. Troxell tells of the experience of a group of tourists, cloud-bound on the summit of Pike's Peak, huddled about the fireplace in the block-house: "It was suggested that we sing some popular melody. A voice began one of the many sentimental songs of the day; but few knew enough of it to join in, so the singer was left to finish it alone. Then some one began to sing softly, 'Nearer, My God, to Thee,' and before the second line was ended it seemed as if all who had been strangers now felt at home; and, for the time being, the place seemed like a very Bethel." Before long the mists rolled away and "before us stretched the most wonderful of views."

This hymn is remembered as the dying prayer of our martyred President McKinley.

99. Hark! the Herald Angels Sing

CHARLES WESLEY, 1707-1788

FOR years the only hymn of Charles Wesley's admitted to the *Book of Common Prayer* of the Church of England was this Christmas hymn. This was true in spite of the fact that, as an ordained clergyman of that denomination, he was the greatest hymn-writer ever produced by the Church of England. But, of course, Charles Wesley and his brother, John Wesley, belong to Methodism as well. Until death came to them they remained clergymen of the Established Church. The great religious movement founded by John Wesley, and inspired by the hymns of Charles Wesley, and known therefore as the Wesleyan Revival, was intended to quicken the spiritual work of their church. But, besides doing this, it developed into organized Methodism as a separate church, and as such has proved to be a tremendous religious force in the world.

This Christmas hymn was first written in 1739 and first published the same year in *Hymns and Sacred Poems* by John and Charles Wesley, their first joint hymnal; and it began with the lines:

> Hark! how all the welkin rings,
> Glory to the King of kings.

Many revisions have been made in the original hymn, some of which are contained in our most modern hymnals. This hymn has been more widely published in hymn books than any other by Charles Wesley, and is one of the most beloved hymns in the English language. It gives such clear utterance in poetic form to the doctrines of the incarnation that the full meaning of the birth of Christ fairly sings its way into the hearts and memories of those who worship.

100. Awake, My Soul, and With the Sun

Bishop Thomas Ken, 1637-1711

When Thomas Ken was a child both of his parents died and Izaac Walton, husband of his older sister, Ann, became his guardian. At the age of fourteen he became a scholar in Winchester College, and the affection which he formed for Winchester in those early school days exerted a great influence in his subsequent life and in the writing of this greatest of morning hymns. Five years after he had won the degree of B. A. from New College, Oxford, he was made a Fellow of Winchester and later chaplain to Morley, Bishop of Winchester.

This renewal of his association with the scenes of his school life at Winchester and his deep concern for the spiritual life of the boys then in school led him to write three hymns especially for them, for "Morning," "Midnight," and "Evening," each one concluding with what we call the Long-Meter Doxology (*q. v.,* p. 86). The greatest of these was the Morning Hymn.

Ken united fearlessness and gentleness in his saintly character. Macaulay said that he came "as near as human infirmity permits to the ideal perfection of Christian virtue." When chaplain to Princess Mary at The Hague he was dismissed for condemning the immorality at Court; and for similar courage on another occasion Charles II made him Bishop of Bath and Wells. James imprisoned him in the Tower of London and William III removed him from his see for not complying against his conscience with the royal will.

When at last in 1711 he died, he was buried according to his wish at Frome "under the east window of the chancel, just at sunrising," as his sorrowing friends sang his own morning hymn, "Awake, My Soul, and With the Sun."

101. God Be With You Till We Meet Again

JEREMIAH EAMES RANKIN, 1828-1904

DOCTOR RANKIN, a native of New Hampshire and a graduate of Middlebury College, for many years held the pastorates successively of several prominent Congregational churches in New England and Washington, D. C., until 1889, when he became president of Howard University.

While pastor of a Congregational church in Washington, D. C., he became so impressed with the etymology of the farewell greeting, "good-by," which really means "God be with you," that he determined that a hymn should be wrought out of this beautiful idea. So he came to write "God be with you till we meet again."

When he had written the first stanza he sent it to two different composers, one quite famous, the other little known, each of whom wrote a tune for it. He chose the tune of the latter, W. G. Tomer, who was then teaching school in Washington. Doctor Rankin submitted it to his organist, J. W. Bishoff, a musical editor, and Bishoff approved of it, making certain changes in it. In the words of the author: "It was sung for the first time one evening in the First Congregational Church, in Washington, of which I was then the pastor and Mr. Bishoff the organist. I attributed its popularity in no little part to the music to which it is set. It was a wedding of words and music."

God himself alone knows how many, many times this hymn has been sung in parting by friends who have never again met upon this earth. But no happier farewell can be uttered by Christians than the simple wish, "God be with you till we meet again."

INDEX

INDEX

We S... at Easter 7...